HUGH ELLIS AND KATE

ENGLISH PLANNING IN CRISIS

10 Steps to a Sustainable Future

POLICY PRESS SHORTS POLICY & PRACTICE

First published in Great Britain in 2016 by

Policy Press
University of Bristol
1-9 Old Park Hill
Bristol
BS2 8BB
UK
t: +44 (0)117 954 5940
pp-info@bristol.ac.uk
www.policypress.co.uk

North America office:
Policy Press
c/o The University of Chicago Press
1427 East 60th Street
Chicago, IL 60637, USA
t: +1 773 702 7700
f: +1 773 702 9756
sales@press.uchicago.edu
www.press.uchicago.edu

© Policy Press 2016

British Library Cataloguing in Publication Data
A catalogue record for this book is available from the British Library.

Library of Congress Cataloging-in-Publication Data
A catalog record for this book has been requested.

ISBN 978-1-4473-3034-9 (paperback)
ISBN 978-1-4473-3247-3 (ePub)
ISBN 978-1-4473-3248-0 (Mobi)

The rights of Hugh Ellis and Kate Henderson to be identified as the authors of this work has been asserted by them in accordance with the Copyright, Designs and Patents Act 1988.

Cover design by Policy Press
Image: www.alamy.com
Printed and bound in Great Britain by CMP, Poole
Policy Press uses environmentally responsible print partners

Contents

Acknowledgements

English planning in crisis comes out of multiple collaborations and research projects that we have had the opportunity to work on at the Town and Country Planning Association (TCPA), from pan-European projects on spatial planning and sustainable energy through to the Planning4People education and advocacy project and the Association's ongoing Garden Cities campaign. We would like to thank all of our fantastic colleagues and the Board of Trustees at the TCPA for their enthusiasm for planning and belief in the utopian tradition. While drawing heavily on work undertaken at the TCPA, the views expressed are ours, and not necessarily those of the Association.

We are incredibly lucky to have such supportive family and friends. In particular we would like to thank Samantha Wood, Hannah Henderson, Fiona Mannion, Julie Dixon and Chris Ellis for their comments and encouragement. Their wise edits and constructive criticism definitely helped shape the book for the better.

Thanks to the brilliant team at Policy Press for supporting us in writing this second book. Particular thanks to Laura Vickers our Editor for her enthusiasm and support.

We are grateful to James and Ceri for their patience and understanding, which we know we have tested at times. Thank you for all your love and support. Thanks to Samuel, Bethan and Owain for giving us hope and inspiration about the future.

Finally, our thanks and love go to John Henderson and Ann Syrett, this book is dedicated to you both.

Foreword

Baroness Kay Andrews, OBE

Planning is about making places and shaping the future. It has a profound impact on our lives in every way possible. Planning is not simply about approving housing units, it is about determining whether communities thrive or not. Planning is about our collective future: whether we are resilient or vulnerable, healthy or unwell, productive or idle. Of all the public services, planning is the one defined by its concern not just for this generation, but for the long-term welfare of future generations. In 1947 the Town and Country Planning Act took its place alongside the NHS Act, the Education Act and the National Insurance Act as the foundation for a new, more prosperous and more socially just society.

But planning for the future is under assault as never before. The recent report of the House of Lords Select Committee on the Built Environment concluded: 'as a nation, our aspirations for the quality of the built environment have been routinely too low. Only the Government can set a more ambitious path and we urge this government to do so.'

This book records with stark clarity the decline of planning in England and the gulf between the aspirations of the founders of the planning movement and its current principles and practice. The authors also offer us the passionate hope that we can rebuild the institutions, knowledge and commitment of the planning service. They make clear that, with the talent and the vision we already have among our planners, architects and engineers, we can make much better places in the future. We can do this by recognising that the best places to live are those which understand how arts, heritage and culture enrich our lives and create a sense of belonging. The best places understand the need for rich habitats, and green space too, as well as a paramount emphasis on quality and design, inclusion and resilience. In short, this book offers a prescription for the sorts of communities we would all choose to live in.

Baroness Andrews
House of Lords, London
March 2016

Note

[1] House of Lords Select Committee on National Policy for the Built Environment (2016) *Report of Session 2015–16: Building better places*, 19 February, www.publications.parliament.uk/pa/ld201516/ldselect/ldbuilt/100/100.pdf

ONE

Introduction

This book has two simple messages. Firstly, the rich utopian tradition that underpinned the town planning movement in England is dead. It now needs wholesale recreation. Secondly, if we are to achieve this renaissance we need positive and creative ideas that make a real difference to people's lives.

This book is part manifesto for the future of England and part elegy for the wider western utopian tradition, a tradition we celebrate in 2016 with the 500th anniversary of the publication of Thomas More's Utopia.[1] With a kind of ironic symmetry we will mark this date in England with the abandonment of any commitment to the high ideals that drove so much progressive change over the last 150 years. In a debate marked by a rich mix of apathy and political hypocrisy, England will bury these utopian ideals just at the moment when we, and wider world, need them most. The external challenges intensify as fast as we destroy the tools we need to deal with them. From the historic agreement at the United Nations Paris Climate Conference[2] in November 2015 to the severe flooding in Cumbria in December 2015,[3] from the growing levels of homelessness in England to the greatest mass migration in Europe since 1945, we are unprepared and ill equipped.

The notion of sustainable development in town planning, the supposed foundation of the system, is now completely devalued, appearing at the table occasionally like Banquo's ghost to remind planners of what they used to believe in. Planning has been subject to regulatory capture, with those whom it was meant to regulate now dictating its form, policy and implementation. It has become fashionable to blame those parts of the private sector development community who have done well out of these changes. That is an easy analysis, but it is both wrong and not the purpose of this book. In fact some parts of the private sector have done very badly out the government's reforms on a range of policies, most notably those working with innovative place-making technologies in energy efficiency,[4] renewable energy[5] and flood resilience. The responsibility for the purpose and implementation of planning policy lies with government; and with those who elected them. It is for government to make the rules, and to preserve and promote the public interest.

Why history matters: the utopian test

The history of utopian thought is vital as an inspiration for how high ideals can be made real, with enormous benefit to society. But the ideals of a collective future in which resources are more evenly distributed between current and future generations is deeply unpopular among the minority of individuals and corporations who own most of the Earth's resources. The UK is a particularly unequal society, compared to other developed countries. The Equality Trust has revealed the growing gap in wealth inequality, with the richest 10% of households holding 45% of all wealth, whereas the poorest 50% of households own just 8.7%.[6]

Instead of building on the legacy of success of the planning movement, over the last 50 years we have instead chosen to focus overwhelmingly on the shortcomings of the system, to the point that they have become a mythology of failure. Worse still, we have chosen to forget our past and no longer teach or debate the utopian tradition that was once a dominant strand of public discourse. In the process, hope of an alternative future founded on social justice and equality has been extinguished. The utopian tradition is a rich, diverse, creative and, above all, humanist tradition, rejecting dogma and stressing the importance of individuals and community action. It is just as challenging for the Left in politics as it is for the Right.

Our history really does matter. And while there is nothing automatically important about an anniversary, it does allow for brief moment of reflection on where we came from. Thomas More finished *Utopia* in 1516 at time of political turmoil in Europe and personal turmoil in terms of his career choice. One might conclude that *Utopia* was More's farewell to freedom of thought before he began his meteoric rise as one of the highest servants of the Tudor court.[7]

England in 1516 was a nation surrounded by European conflict over power and, particularly, commercial competition between the growing mercantile classes of Europe. In the English kingdom there was transformational economic change on the land, with landowners beginning the process of enclosure to create pasture for that most profitable of commodities, wool. Peasants were moved off the land, rents were raised and a very few landowners, including the church, made colossal fortunes. So, while there is a long-running debate about More's intentions in writing *Utopia* – satire, intellectual flight of fancy – it remains the most powerful of a whole number of contemporary critiques of Tudor society. It derives its power from a simple and enduring truth that critique is not enough. Real change is driven by the audacity of seeking alternatives, and real radicalism by making these a practical reality that can clearly make people's lives better.

Utopia is composed of two books. Book 1 is nothing more than a coded demolition job of many of the political ills of the Tudor court. Book 2 is unique in the scope of its bold vision for the future. In a hundred or so pages, More sets out a network of cities and discuses equality, health, well-being, education, governance, food production and the military. Written 500 years ago, it is not surprising that some of it is downright weird by our standards, but it is a more comprehensive picture of the city-state than anything we have now, and considerably more coherent. It is a reaction to the absolute monarchy and extreme inequality of Tudor England, but it still feels remarkably modern. It suggests that cities should be obligated to support each other in times of crisis, a principle England might well wish to adopt now to help deal with the challenges facing our communities today, such as flooding and rising homelessness.

More's *Utopia* is relevant today because land is power, and remains so. The battle between the collective control of land and individual control is as bitter now as ever. The modern fire-sale of public assets, such as public land, and passage of vast sums to property interest through deregulation, such as permitted development rights, would have sat entirely comfortably in the Tudor court of Henry VIII. The argument is the same. Who gets the benefit of land? Who wins the argument over the primary assets of the Earth – assets which are both scarce and finite? In short, how are we to live?

More's *Utopia* is so enduring because it is a brilliant illustration of an alternative society and it opened the door that many others have walked through to enrich and reinforce the utopian tradition. From political activist and religious reformer Gerard Winstanley, in the English Civil War, to the romantic poets; from industrial philanthropists, such as Cadbury at Bournville, to the Chartist land movement; from the first Town Planning Act in 1909 to the triumph of the 1946 New Towns Act; *Utopia* was the inspiration. It made ambitious dreams somehow normal; it gave people courage to challenge powerful injustice. There was a good reason why the book was reprinted many times in the unique decade of 1890s, when the utopian tradition made great intellectual and artistic progress, framing the beginning of the garden city movement and a century dominated by extraordinary social progress.

Before there is any anxiety that *English planning in crisis* is an extended history lesson we can be clear that it is not. However, the utopian tradition contains the instructions for our future. So, to be clear, there are two reasons why 2016 is such a milestone. It marks the final fall from grace of this vital tradition and it marks the beginning of its resurrection, not because anyone may wish it so, but because it provides the progressive tools to counter the most pressing threats which our society confronts.

So where does this leave us? The utopian tradition provides a way of thinking: ambitious, challenging and practical. It provides us with the key principles upon which to found action and, above all, social justice through the fair distribution of political rights and economic resources. It suggests a conception of human beings as capable of creative, cooperative work. It provides a strongly humanist view of human needs for art, work and fellowship as well as material well-being. Finally, it provides a fiercely forensic concern with what works and what doesn't, and so a tendency to avoid dogma and a focus on robust evidence.

You might be wondering how any of these ideas relate to the current planning system in England. You will search in vain for Thomas More, John Ruskin or William Morris in our National Planning Policy Framework – the guiding framework for planning in England. This is very odd, because talking about planning without them is like talking about physics without referencing Einstein. The Utopians recognised, in founding the town planning movement, that the future had to be organised and that disorganisation kept us poor and divided. They saw, as we do, that planning was a broad activity relating to all aspects of social organisation. That, after all, is what a garden city is meant be. So, while the current planning system is failing to meet the needs of so many people in society, the utopian tradition asks us to raise our sights, redefining spatial or urban planning as a much wider and exciting endeavour of shaping the future for the common good. It involves, as it did in 1900, a rich cross sector of disciplines, and when it is fully restored it will be the most important function in our society.

And will this transformation come about by sudden mass readership of *Utopia*? No. It will come about because the disorganisation of society is driving poor outcomes for people. In Cumbria, where some communities have experienced severe and repeated flooding, they know they need a plan for their collective future. Quite soon we will recognise that the fate of the people in Cumbria, and the fates of millions of people around the globe, result from a huge collective failure to plan for the future based on the evidence about climate change that has confronted us clearly for a quarter of a century.

Who cares about utopia today?

The lack of civil-society debate about the decline in planning is one of the great curiosities of the political world since 2010. But then it is hard to blame people for not being more concerned when we have failed to communicate the rich and positive stream of alternatives to many of our current problems. It is like being asked what you want to eat in a restaurant without being shown the menu. If you are homeless, like the 59,000 homeless households currently living in temporary accommodation in England,[8] or you are facing eviction because you asked your private landlord to fix a problem in your home, like 200,000 people this year,[9] then you might not have time or space for utopia.

Across England, there is little sign of social unrest or even mild political discontent. Housing is being built, unemployment is at moderately low levels and the population is more concerned with deciding whether to be European rather than engaging with the apparently mind-bogglingly dull prospect of planning our future. But if you look a little deeper something is changing. The agreement at the United Nations Climate Conference in Paris at the end of 2015 has brought back to life the centrality of climate change to our future and reminds us that our current political and economic system has brought us to the brink of planetary disaster. The impacts are no longer abstract, with severe weather hitting us hard in ways that were pretty much predicted 25 years ago. Those climate deniers who have done so much to damage our rational response to reducing greenhouse gas emissions and building community resilience are quieter now as our – now enhanced – flood defences fail to cope with the sheer quantity of water falling out of the sky. People and places are hurting, their economies damaged and morale tested because of our failure to plan.

Inequality is a growing issue expressed in access to decent housing, in income and health inequality and in the kinds of economic future we are creating for places. The housing crisis in England is affecting people right across the country. Parts of the country face a chronic undersupply of affordable homes because we have failed to build enough new homes to meet demand for decades. In other parts of

England, the challenge is regeneration of our existing communities and the quality of existing social housing. Poor-quality and insecure housing has an acute impact on the health, well-being and education of those in greatest housing need. Our inadequate supply of housing also reduces labour mobility, thereby undermining the ability of our towns and cities to attract new business. For example 'three in five young teachers say they will leave London in the next five years due to unaffordable housing', according to a 2015 survey by the National Union of Teachers.[10]

While the housing crisis has risen up the political agenda, the government's priority since 2015 has been on supporting homeownership and reducing the housing benefit bill. However, following the extension of the Right to Buy to housing association tenants, being introduced in the Housing and Planning Bill 2015, and cuts to rental income from social housing which will take effect from April 2016, social housing will be a far smaller player in the housing market; but it doesn't have to be this way. As Nick Raynsford, a former Minister for Housing and Planning, highlighted in 2013, 'We are spending around £25 billion each year on housing subsidies. But around £23 billion is going on Housing Benefit, and only a little under £2 billion a year is supporting social and affordable housebuilding. So it is not the case that we do not have the money.'[11]

Concern is also growing for the kinds of business we are promoting in England. Some businesses have questionable working practices, such as employing staff on zero hours contracts.[12] It has come to exemplify a low-wage economy in which taxpayers have to support the profits of private sector companies through working tax credits and other welfare benefits.[13] Is this really the economy that will secure our future?

Technological change is moving at a fast pace and provides new opportunities for civic engagement through social media, but there are also questions about the impact of technology on employment in the future. Technology is amoral and, while it is driving productivity and wealth for some, it is also leaving many people and communities behind. For example, internet shopping has created new business opportunities for both big businesses and people working at home from their kitchen tables, but its success is also partly responsible for the decline of so many of our high streets across towns and cities in England. The British Retail Consortium has produced evidence to suggest that 900,000 UK retail jobs could be lost by 2025.[14] When we look to the future, we need to consider whether continued technological advancement and mechanisation will remove many of the existing jobs in the economy over the next 20 years and, if so, how our young people are to earn a living. The point here is not to plead for a bizarre 'back to the land' movement but to ask, as we did for 500 years, who is this change for? Who benefits? How can these changes be put to work for the collective welfare of society and, most important, to meet the challenges that could hold back progress to a genuinely sustainable future?

English planning in crisis

In *Rebuilding Britain*, published in 2014, we set out the fundamental contribution that the utopian and town planning tradition had made to our society and how such ideas are perfectly relevant to help us tackle the key problems we faced. This was, above all, a debate about recreating hope and redirecting our resources to building a collective future based on human well-being and social justice. This was at a time when, despite the decline of planning, there was still a sense of being able to restore the planning system as a major foundation of public policy in the creation of the good society. The many problems that the planning system faced were not impossible to fix. Unfortunately, in the two years since then many of the policies and approaches that could have helped build a more sustainable future – onshore wind energy, zero-carbon homes or social housing for example – have become increasingly difficult to deliver through the planning system because of government policy changes and further deregulation. One of the main motivations for publishing *English planning in crisis* is to record the scale of this shift in English planning policy and values – particularly key polices on climate change and social housing – and to try to keep alive the prospect of something different. The book reveals some of the drivers behind the radical changes in policy and tracks how planning was transformed from a visionary utopian and progressive social force into little more than a residual form of land licensing.

While Part One of this book provides an analysis of the crisis in English planning today, Part Two sets out what we might do about this through exploring ten ideas for how the system might be transformed, offering practical help for the future. Like *Rebuilding Britain*, this book is underpinned by the values of utopian tradition, the values that shaped the planning movement and continue to inform it in many nations across the world. Those values are founded on social justice, on fair rights to participate in decisions and, crucially, on the fair distribution of the resources that arise from the development of land and primary resources. These solutions are founded on the fierce assessment and rational application of evidence – what works and what does not. From Ebenezer Howard onwards, the Utopians have had this key practical test at the front of their campaigns and combined it with a passion to get on with the job. We need to recapture this passion, pragmatism and vision.

Notes

[1] More, T. (1516) *Utopia*, London: Penguin Classics, 1993 edn, Ronald Herder.

[2] United Nations Framework Convention on Climate Change (2015) *Paris Climate Change Conference – November 2015*, UNFCC website, http://unfccc.int/meetings/paris_nov_2015/meeting/8926.php.

[3] Met Office (2015) *Flooding in Cumbria December 2015*, Met Office website, www.metoffice.gov.uk/climate/uk/interesting/december2015.

[4] Murray, J. (2015) 'National Insulation Association says 2,000 green jobs lost due to energy efficiency policy "void"', Business Green website, www.businessgreen.com/bg/analysis/2432168/national-insulation-association-says-2-000-green-jobs-lost-due-to-energy-efficiency-policy-void.

[5] Macalister, T. (2015) 'UK solar panel subsidy cuts branded "huge and misguided"', 17 December, *Guardian*, www.theguardian.com/business/2015/dec/17/uk-solar-panel-subsidies-slashed-paris-climate-change.

[6] Equalities Trust (2016) *The scale of economic inequality in the UK*, Equalities Trust website, https://www.equalitytrust.org.uk/scale-economic-inequality-uk.

[7] Ackroyd, P. (1998) *The life of Thomas More*, London: Vintage.

[8] Shelter (2016) *Households in temporary accommodation*, Shelter website, http://england.shelter.org.uk/campaigns_/why_we_campaign/housing_facts_and_figures/subsection?section=temporary_accomodation#hf_1.

[9] Shelter (2016) *Safe and decent home*, Shelter website, http://england.shelter.org.uk/campaigns_/why_we_campaign/improving_private_renting/safe_and_decent_homes.

[10] NUT (2015) *Standing up for London's education*, https://www.teachers.org.uk/files/london-manifesto-16pp-a5-10327.pdf.

[11] Raynsford, N. (2013) *T&CP Tomorrow Series Paper 15: The Challenge of the Housing Crisis*, London: TCPA www.tcpa.org.uk/data/files/Nick_Raynsford_TS.pdf.

[12] Ruddick, G. (2015) 'Sports Direct denies "Dickensian practices" in face of investor revolt', 9 September, *Guardian*, www.theguardian.com/business/2015/sep/09/sports-direct-investors-revolt-against-chairman-and-pay-policy.

[13] BBC (2015) '"Dickensian" protest against zero-hour contracts at Sports Direct', BBC website, 9 September, www.bbc.co.uk/news/uk-england-derbyshire-34202858.

[14] Ahmed, K. (2016) '900,000 UK retail jobs could be lost by 2025, warns BRC', BBC website, www.bbc.co.uk/news/business-35681474.

PART ONE

TWO

Utopia abandoned?

In this chapter we look at the decline of planning in England and set out the key reform measures introduced since 2015. The process of the decline of planning in England did not start in 2015 or in 2010, and the reasons why it came about are complicated. We recognise that the current government is not solely responsible for extinguishing the utopian values that once underpinned the town planning movement. One cannot honestly say, that for a generation, planning has always upheld beauty in design or social inclusion. Planning has not always secured the most basic infrastructure provision, such as enough school places or capacity on our overcrowded road and rail networks. However, planning did intervene to secure mixed-use developments and, through planning obligations, it helped secure a proportion of social and genuinely affordable homes. It has also continued to make a real contribution to the nation by, for example, protecting some of our most important landscapes, but these tend to be legacy issues resulting from designations, such as National Parks, made 70 years ago. Although there was a brief period of resurgence around spatial planning and sustainable development in the 2000s, it was very short lived. Strategic planning in England, for example, lasted from 2005 until 2010, which now looks like the blink of an eye.

Since 1970, when the last post-war New Town was designated, planning has been unable to deliver high-quality, large-scale new communities based on the garden city principles. Above all, town planning is no longer an active movement for visionary and holistic place-making, which was its core inspiration and primary function.

At its worst, planning now creates bolt-on housing estates without social facilities and infrastructure provision, little or no public green space or private gardens, homes with tiny rooms on the inside and that on the outside reflect repetitive design, with no thought for local distinctiveness. When compared to the housing that the industrial philanthropists built, the model villages at Bournville and Saltaire, the garden cities at Letchworth and Welwyn, or even interwar council housing, we have gone backwards in the most spectacular manner. So, while we can be certain about how far we have fallen, it remains to try to understand why this happened and why the public and the built-environment professions didn't speak up in defence of the value of planning to society, the environment and the economy. However, before we explore the questions around the lack of debate about the decline of planning, let's first look at some of the key reforms introduced in the period preceding the UK general election in 2015 and what has happened since.

Planning reform at the end of the Coalition government

In the year before the general election the Coalition government deregulated many forms of policy on planning, housing and the built environment. For example, just before the election in April 2015, the Code for Sustainable Homes was withdrawn, marking the end of comprehensive standards covering a full range of environmental and design issues.[1] The Deregulation Act, which received Royal Assent in March 2015, made changes to the local plan-making process, meaning that local planning authorities were no longer able to include 'any additional local technical standards or requirements relating to the construction, internal layout or performance of new dwellings'[2] in their emerging plans.

By 2015, the National Planning Policy Framework (NPPF), introduced in 2012, had really started to have a demonstrable impact.

The NPPF's focus on housing numbers has undoubtedly been a success for government – in the 12 months to March 2015, 261,000 homes were approved in England, which is more than the estimated demographic need of 220,000 new homes per annum;[3,4] but this achievement of quantity of consents was in stark contrast to the quality of what was consented to and to the actual delivery of homes by some parts of the house-building industry.

There are also significant issues of delivery of some policies in the NPPF, so that while the document contains important policy on good design and climate change mitigation, for example, there is little sign that such policy is being implemented on the ground. The reason why this is happening is because the NPPF places highly variable weight on differing policy objectives; the viability test and five-year land supply are pre-eminent tests, while good design and climate change mitigation are not.

The viability test applies to all policy requirements set out by councils and communities in their local and neighbourhood plans. The test is based on a straightforward residual valuation of development in order to 'provide a competitive return to willing developers and land owners'.[5] This means that many policies with long-term benefits can be ruled out of local plans if they compromise a developer's profit margins. As a consequence of the viability test, the wider and long-term social and economic benefits of measures such as Sustainable Urban Drainage in reducing insurance costs by preventing flooding cannot be accounted for.

This is just one example; policy on a whole series of other vital public interest outcomes has also been downgraded or removed, particularly in relation to affordable homes and building standards. For example, 53% of local authorities surveyed across England in February 2015 identified the viability test in the NPPF as negatively impacting on their ability to deliver affordable and social homes, compared with just 14% who felt that the viability test helped, according to the Association for Public Sector Excellence (APSE).[6] Exactly the same scenario applies to the national buildings standards framework, introduced in 2015, in relation to space standards and Lifetime Homes. Local government is not obliged to adopt even these minimum standards, but if it does they must pass the viability test. A 2016 report by the House of Lords Select Committee on a National Policy for the Built Environment stated: 'We believe that this is a short-sighted approach. Lifetime Homes have the potential to ensure that our built environment is better placed to cope with a changing population. The additional cost appears, to us, to be relatively marginal when compared to the wider social and economic benefits.'[7] The Lords' Built Environment Committee has also said that there is a 'compelling case to revise national planning policy and guidance to ensure that individual viability assessments do not systematically undermine the delivery of affordable housing and other planning obligations'.

Planning in England since the 2015 general election

One of the many difficulties about recording the decline of English town planning is that the government is constantly making changes to the process. One might conclude that this continuous tinkering with planning has further discredited the system, undoubtedly adding to the confusion and discontent that surround it.

The Housing and Planning Bill, introduced by the government in the autumn of 2015, which is being debated in the House of Lords as we write this book, signals the end of social housing in England and sets out further radical reform of the planning system. Two of the measures included in the Housing and Planning Bill illustrate the scale of the changes to the planning system. The first is the introduction of 'zonal' planning based on international experience, and the second paves the way to the privatisation of the planning application process.

The government has sought to downplay these measures, but if they are made law as currently drafted, they would represent a fundamental change to what is left of the planning system in England. The Housing and Planning Bill includes a measure called 'permission in principle' and is based on a zonal planning model. Zonal planning was first suggested by the Chancellor of the Exchequer in July 2015, when he published the Productivity Plan.[8] However, it appears that the government carried out no analysis of international zonal systems before they were included in the draft legislation, and yet zonal planning – that is, permission given through the plan – has a highly variable international reputation and has been used in some US cities to reinforce racial segregation.[9] On the other hand, the adoption of a European-style zonal planning system, along the lines of that operating in the Netherlands, could be potentially positive – but only if the lessons to be learnt from the Dutch system are fully implemented and the same ethos is adopted – and there is no indication that they will be. The idea of permission being granted with the adoption of the plan is a key part of the Dutch system, but so too is the idea of the public sector as lead developers, backed by public sector investment, which is the opposite of the current, developer-led model in England.

The government has also put forward measures to privatise the planning application process, arguing that this is only a pilot project, but presumably it reflects a direction of travel and a commitment to the introduction of commercial values and competition into a key part of local governance. The proposed legislation would break new ground by allowing a developer to appoint an 'alternative provider' to process their planning application.[10] Under the system proposed, the consultant employed by the developer would be required to make judgements including: which neighbours to consult, how to interpret the views of internal and external consultees, whether concerns expressed by neighbours are relevant, which policies are relevant to the decision, and to make a recommendation on whether the planning application should be approved and, if so, what conditions should be applied. The local authority would retain the responsibility for the final decision.

While some local authorities – for example Salford City Council and North East Lincolnshire Council – are already using private sector consultancies to deliver all or the majority of their planning services through outsourcing deals,[11] the new model being proposed in the Housing and Planning Bill is different because the private firm is chosen by the applicant, not the council. Whether this route will be seen as legitimate and independent by the public is highly questionable. Councillor Martin Tett, Vice-Chair of the Local Government

Association's Environment, Economy, Housing and Transport Board, and Leader of Buckinghamshire County, told the House of Commons Communities and Local Government Select Committee in February 2016 that this measure creates a 'massive potential for conflicts of interest ... if it is a controversial application I can see all sorts of grounds for potential judicial review, which could actually slow down the planning process rather than speed it up'.[12]

The government's 'alternative provider' proposal could fundamentally change the public service ethos of the planning system, with the potential to damage its integrity and credibility in the eyes of the public. In any case, the changes being proposed by government require proper public debate and scrutiny, yet these measures have been brought forward without any public consultation. They were introduced after the detailed examination of the Housing and Planning Bill by the House of Commons, which meant that the government bypassed vital aspects of parliamentary democracy. The government has also been widely criticised for holding the first parliamentary debate on these measures at 3:00 in the morning.[13] It is not hard to understand why the public and civil society groups are not engaged in this debate, when they had no way of knowing that it was happening.

In addition to the Housing and Planning Bill, since 2015 the government has also made permanent many of the changes that it said were temporary measures to deal with the economic crisis, such as permitted development (the conversion of commercial buildings into homes without needing planning permission). The government has also abandoned other commitments; for example, in July 2015 it cancelled the 2016 zero-carbon commitment, which has stark consequences for our ability to mitigate dangerous climate change, leaving no trajectory for ensuring that our homes and offices will be fit for the future.[14]

The great devolution dance

The deregulation of planning has gone hand in hand with the rapid devolution of some planning powers to parts of England.

Describing this process is very challenging, partly because at the time of writing this book the devolution deals are still being negotiated and partly because it illustrates the deeply conflicted nature of the government's attitude to governance and power. For example, at one end of the scale, the Housing and Planning Bill centralises a whole series of controls over local government on the process and outcomes of the planning system and gives these powers to the Secretary of State. These include the requirements for councils to produce local plans by 2017 or government will ensure that plans are produced for them, and new duties on councils to promote Starter Homes, a new form of subsidised homeownership discussed below. At the other end of the scale, the government wants to simplify and speed up the neighbourhood planning system through the Housing and Planning Bill. Neighbourhood planning, a community tier of planning introduced in the Localism Act in 2011, has proved very popular, and by late 2015 the government reported that 'over 1,700 communities, representing over 8 million people across the country are now neighbourhood planning'.[15]

The same contrast is illustrated in the devolution debate, where, having abolished English regional strategic planning, the government is now reinventing it through a series of devolution deals that will result in a new geography of local government, with new combined authorities acting at city-region or sub-regional scales.

Devolution of power is normally perceived as a progressive policy and, if done well, could create, for example, powerful municipalities and cities with a much stronger foundation for local autonomy over planning and housing. Unfortunately for the future of England, devolution is progressing in a chaotic and opaque manner. Devolution is not proceeding after a plentiful public debate, or after a Royal Commission, which might have set out the evidence base and principles. As a result, many people remain unaware of the government's flagship policy, the Northern Powerhouse, with 44% of adults having never heard of it.[16] Each devolution deal encompasses differing agreements on aspects of the devolution of central government spending, powers and governance. This results in a highly variable picture across England, with city-regions like Greater Manchester leading the way, taking power over healthcare provision and creating a city-wide planning strategy, while other places, particularly rural areas outside city regions, are struggling to define both boundaries and powers. Above all, it is the governance and accountability of the new bodies that raises the most concern. Unlike Greater London, upon which the powers are modelled, there is no comprehensive and detailed governance framework and no equivalent of the Greater London Assembly to hold the powers of combined authorities and mayors to account. Instead, the new framework rests on indirect democracy in the hands of the constituent local authority council leaders, which is, and will rapidly be perceived to be, lacking in transparency and accountability.

The future of social housing hangs in the balance

Since 2010, the government has deregulated planning and reduced investment in social and genuinely affordable homes, in the hope that the private sector would substantially fill the gap. The results have been deeply disappointing, not only in what has been delivered – as in the example of the extremely small, 13.1 square-metre flats for sale in London[17] – but in the widening gap between what is being approved through the planning system and what is actually being built.

Following the general election in 2015, the future of social housing hangs in the balance. At the time of writing this book the government is bringing forward proposals in the Housing and Planning Bill focused on increasing homeownership through extending the Right to Buy to housing association tenants.[18] The Right to Buy, originally introduced in 1980, gave council tenants the right to buy the homes they had previously rented. As part of the negotiations between the housing association sector, led by their representative body the National Housing Federation, and the government, it has agreed a voluntary deal to extend the Right to Buy to 1.3 million housing association tenants. The scheme will be funded by forcing councils to sell off high-value council houses when they become vacant. In early 2016 the Local Government Association (LGA) has '... forecast that 66,000 council homes will be sold to tenants under the existing Right to Buy scheme by the end of the decade with current complex rules and restrictions making it difficult for councils to rapidly replace the majority of these homes sold.... The LGA predicts councils could then be forced to sell a further 22,000 "high value" homes in order to fund plans to extend the scheme to housing association tenants ...The LGA is warning that some new housing measures, such as the loss of £2.2 billion from council housing budgets by 2020 as a result of social housing rent cuts, risk making building any replacements all but impossible. It estimates that 80,000 of these 88,000 homes sold under Right to Buy by 2020 will not be replaced as a result.'[19]

The extension of the Right to Buy to housing association tenants has the potential to transform socially and economically diverse communities into exclusively wealthy ones. For example, Bournville Village Trust has issued a stark warning that the Right to Buy would 'immediately lead to a reduction in affordable housing in Bournville where there is simply no remaining physical capacity to build replacement homes'.[20] Bournville Village Trust was originally created in 1900 to manage the estate and today it manages 8,950 homes in Birmingham and Shropshire. In response to the proposals in the Housing and Planning Bill the Trust added: 'selling social housing in Bournville would go directly against the wishes of our Quaker founder – philanthropist, chocolate-maker and one of the country's most prominent and famous entrepreneurs – George Cadbury, whose vision was to create a village where a mixture of people, whatever their economic background, could enjoy high-quality housing. The introduction of Right to Buy at Bournville Village Trust would also inevitably lead to the "gentrification" of this part of Birmingham, which would completely undermine the original vision for the village.'

Another government initiative to support greater levels of homeownership is the Starter Homes policy, which is also being legislated for in the Housing and Planning Bill and supported by government investment announced in the Chancellor's Autumn Statement and Spending Review in November 2015. Starter Homes are designed to support homeownership for people under the age of

40 by offering new-build houses at a discount of at least 20% below their open market value; which is up to £450,000 in London and £250,000 in the rest of England.

Homelessness charity Shelter estimates that while Starter Homes will help some high-earning people in parts of England, middle earners will actually be priced out in 58% of the country, and people on the new 'national living wage' will be priced out in 98% of the country.[21] At the time of writing this book the government is consulting on the NPPF to amend the definition of affordable housing to include Starter Homes; a good example of where some words in English planning policy, such as affordable, now risk meaning their opposite.

Understanding planning reform

The way that language is used in the political debate over planning is crucial in understanding why so much can change with so little apparent public concern. This problem, which the playwright and author Alan Bennett has wisely suggested is now a key part of English politics, is simply one of hypocrisy.[22] In a radio recording first broadcast on BBC Radio 4's The World at One in March 2015, Bennett says that England is best known for its hypocrisy:

> Take London, we extol its beauty and its dignity while at the same time we are happy to sell it off to the highest bidder or the highest builder. We glory in Shakespeare, yet we close our public libraries ... words which start off as good and meaningful, terms like environment and energy saving, rapidly lose any credence because converted into political or PR slogans, ending up the clichéd stuff of an estate agent's brochure, a manual for hypocrisy.

Bennett would make a very good Chief Planner for England, even if the outcomes would be benignly muddled. Given his recent pronouncements. London would contain fewer tall buildings like 20 Fenchurch Street (nicknamed the Walkie Talkie), which was awarded *Building Design* magazine's 2015 Carbuncle Cup for worst building of the year.[23] England would also probably have more energy-efficient buildings and it might even include one or two public libraries. More importantly, Bennett's reflection that the defining English asset is hypocrisy would at least bring some honesty to the debate about our national future. His point is simple: we don't mean what we say and we are too polite or too cowardly to challenge even the most outrageous examples of double-speak. For planning, Bennett's intervention perfectly reflects our current operational principles. Bennett's conclusion that 'what we do best is lip-service' is not just a description of the government's approach to planning, but is in fact the underlying philosophy of a good deal of planning practice.

We talk about sustainable development and place-making while cancelling the zero-carbon homes policy and the Eco-towns Planning Policy Statement and, along with it, the last vestige of any place-making objectives in government policy. We talk about 200,000 affordable starter homes for young people and then redefine affordable to mean housing for sale at 80% of the market price, which in London in 2016 is £450,000. So affordable housing actually means unaffordable housing. The government talks about its green credentials while cancelling support for our most effective forms of renewable energy, such as onshore wind. It is important to be specific about these claims because many students and practitioners of planning read national planning guidance, the NPPF, and discover important content on good design and reducing greenhouse gas emissions.[24] This is true. However, as highlighted earlier in this chapter, the reality is that some parts of the NPPF carry much more legal weight than others because of the way the policy language is constructed. Put simply, some polices in the NPPF, such as the presumption in favour of development, the five-year housing land supply and viability of local plan policy, are pre-eminent policy tests. Councils must address these issues and, if they don't, then they will not have a legally sound local development plan, or they will lose an appeal.

A large proportion of the rest of the NPPF policies are simply 'nice to have' and, crucially, if any are expressed in a local council's plan policy in ways which impact on developers' viability, then they can be struck down by the Planning Inspectorate, the government's executive agency whose job it is to make decisions and approve local authority plans. No plan has failed a soundness test because of its failure to deal with climate change, even though few, if any, local plans comply with NPPF policy on reducing greenhouse emissions. These messages about planning priorities are also made – more or less subtly – by the Department for Communities and Local Government in Ministerial and Chief Planner letters; in 'call in' decisions by the Planning Inspectorate and in speeches made at numerous conferences about ministerial priorities. For example, if we apply the NPPF policy on good design to the vast majority of new housing, does it pass on local distinctiveness or sensitivity to landscape? The answer is depressingly obvious. The NPPF is, to steal Bennett's phrase, the ultimate national 'manual of hypocrisy,' helpfully condensing the double-speak into a bite-size 54 pages so we can be clear that localism means centralism and that the viability of private interests is the overriding objective of planning. Alan Bennett's point is really important to all of us because, put simply, language can no longer be trusted. In understanding planning reform we have to interrogate every syllable and recognise that some words now simply mean their opposite.

Where was the public debate about planning reform?

In *Rebuilding Britain* we set out the long narrative of neoliberal thought that, since the Second World War, has sought to undermine collective and democratic intervention in land to secure the wider public interest. This general picture is useful, but in reality the decline of planning has been driven both by this general trend in politics and by the particular actions and attitudes of key players. These key players range from non-governmental organisations (NGOs) and think-tanks, from professional bodies and academics, to institutional investors in the City of London and, of course, communities and the public. In the past, some of these groups have played a key part in supporting the values of the town planning movement and, in particular, have supported a public-interest view – however vaguely defined – of the purpose of planning. They represented part of the intellectual and moral force that underpinned the practice of town planning. So why hasn't there been much more debate about the decline of planning?

The fact that there is no outcry now among these groups is for four reasons.

Firstly, we have produced no alternative vision, so there is no powerful narrative for the future and no group of thinkers and activists to campaign for such ideas.

Secondly, the needs of many of the players are closely aligned, particularly those of investors, landowners and developers. It is, however, important to recognise that all businesses are different. While some companies take corporate social responsibility seriously and genuinely believe in place-making, others have no interest in the potential benefits, or otherwise, of their activities to society. Investors, landowners and developers have been very effective in lobbying government to seek the general deregulation of planning. Their efforts have focused on reducing and removing environmentally and socially important building standards and significantly reducing the requirement of the private sector to contribute to the delivery of genuinely affordable homes through planning obligations. The government has supported the simple and effective agenda put forward by the private sector, allowing it to build new homes on its own terms, to its own standards and to fixed development models that suit investors, but not necessarily the wider public interest.

Thirdly, private sector consultants often find themselves in a conflicted position. Many planning practices now contain more expertise and skills on planning and place-making than does the denuded public sector. Many consultants have strong ambitions for place-making and strong ethical commitments, but their room for manoeuvre can be limited by the overwhelming weight of their client's brief.

Fourthly, think-tanks are like any part of society, and contain good and bad practice. At their best, they can produce expert evidence and analysis and come up with creative ideas; and at their worst, they produce unevidenced, highly ideological and poor-quality outputs, in the sense of simply not being realistic or workable. Much of what think-tanks have written about planning falls into the latter category. Some think-tanks have been supremely influential in planning and housing reform, not simply through the papers it has produced but because of the exchange of staff, ideas and access with the key parts of government, such as the Prime Minister's office.[25] No student of planning reform should under-estimate the bizarre way in which so called 'blue skies' ideas can arrive in public policy with little or no debate or scrutiny. The culture of seeking ideas only from those who are seen as supporters of a particular ideological view-point is short sighted and leads to poor policy outcomes.

While it is tempting to speak of the 'government's' reforms of planning, in fact the government is a many-headed beast. For example, in England it is the Department for Communities and Local Government (DCLG) that has responsibility for planning, but in practice all key reform decisions are made by the Number 10 Policy Unit, HM Treasury and the Cabinet Office. DCLG is simply a machine for implementation. To understand the reform of planning we need to understand the role of construction and housing in the UK economy and HM Treasury's drive for economic growth. This means that anything, real or imagined, that gets in the way of construction must be eliminated. HM Treasury does not recognise the impacts of abolishing regulation on people and communities, not because it is intentionally uncaring, but because it is ideologically convinced, regardless of which party is in power, that economic growth is the solution to all other social and environmental problems. This is, of course, dangerously simplistic, but it is very powerful. It leads to a political proposition on housing that says if we ask developers to build to decent standards on carbon dioxide emissions or affordable homes, then they simply won't build, so it is better to have something of poor quality than to have nothing at all. This zero-sum analysis of our current development model is again extraordinarily simplistic, but it has proved to be a brilliantly successful piece of politics, sweeping away arguments about place-making, quality, climate change and, ironically, the economic benefits of good development to the wider community. Once the development sector had persuaded HM Treasury that planning regulation was anti-competitive the end game for spatial planning began. HM Treasury has made the case for planning deregulation based on an anti-competitive analysis. This fails to acknowledge the extensive evidence presented to government of the benefits of planning for long-term place-making, human health and economic efficiency.

Deregulation moved ahead fast. There was little or no political resistance, partly because key players did not speak out for the reasons discussed above, but also because spatial planning and place-making proved to have no real major political defenders. The NGO community made up of the social housing sector, environmental and conservation groups and housing and planning charities like the Town and Country Planning Association (TCPA) were fragmented, never speaking with one unified voice. These groups could not find common cause even as they were all suffering from the planning and housing policy-reform process. The social housing sector saw planning as a barrier to delivery, and the environmental sector failed to grasp the vital role of planning and the utopian tradition to holistic, sustainable place-making. It speaks volumes that planning simply wasn't a priority largely because there was no single and unifying idea about what planning was for. John Ruskin would have wept to see the sector – which he inspired – fail to appreciate the interconnections between beauty, nature, social justice and economic efficiency.

Likewise there was, with some notable exceptions, little cross-party understanding or enthusiasm for the values of planning. There was certainly no heavy-weight political advocate for planning, and this is remarkable, given the support for town planning from all sides of politics up into the 1980s. The opposition parties have resisted the government's deregulation of planning, but so far to little effect. The real debate is within the Conservative Party, where there are at least four different ideological positions: (i) an extreme form of free market anti-state ideology, (ii) a traditional conservative and localist view, (iii) a one-nation view with clear social commitment to fairness, and (iv) a business view, happy to see a role for the state if it supports profit maximisation. These different positions are not all incompatible, but the Housing and Planning Bill illustrates how the tensions between them play out. For example, the desire to support communities undertaking neighbourhood planning with legal rights of appeal against developers seems to sit oddly with removing community control from entire categories of development, such as the change of use of buildings that allows for the conversion of commercial buildings into homes without needing planning consent. So far during the debate around the Housing and Planning Bill, the conflicting aspirations for growth at all costs versus strong community-based decision making have been kept under the radar. Who wins this argument will determine the future of the current planning system. This conflict between a drive for growth from the centre of government and local aspirations also helps to explain why neighbourhood planning, the most powerful form of community-based planning ever introduced, and the deregulation of permitted development, which removes the community's voice on major forms of development, can emerge from the same government.

What does the public think about planning?

Today planning issues fill most of the post bags of national and local politicians, but, unlike in the 1980s, there has been only limited discontent over the deregulation of planning. This is partly because, for the reasons already discussed, there is very little public awareness of what has actually happened, and partly because the public reflects the wider decline of planning, with much less public conversation about planning and design than there was 40 or 50 years ago. As we pointed out in *Rebuilding Britain*, people are no less concerned with where they live, but they see this as a personal rather than collective question. Building also takes time, so perhaps in two or three years, when the lack of the most basic social infrastructure begins to bite, people will ask 'how did we let this happen?'

A catalogue of deregulation

We catalogued many aspects of the deregulation of planning in *Rebuilding Britain*, including the end of regional planning and the failure of the 'duty to cooperate', introduced in the 2011 Localism Act, to ensure meaningful strategic planning; but since that time the process has intensified. In March 2015 the TCPA published *The Future of Planning and Place-Making*,[26] which concluded that the English planning system was not fit for purpose and required urgent attention to secure clear, progressive objectives and a logical structure that reflected the functional geography of England. The report concluded that 'England has:

- no effective national spatial planning, with consequent lost opportunities to co-ordinate housing and infrastructure delivery;
- a dysfunctional sub-national planning framework, following the abolition of regional planning and consequent loss of key pertinent data – the 'duty to co-operate' (a mechanism which requires local authorities to consult one another), even where it has been successful in its own terms, has not delivered the benefits of strategic planning;
- a non-spatial NPPF which deprioritises place-making, affordability, equality and inclusion and prioritises the needs of developers and landowners;
- a Local Plan process which, because of inherent flaws in national policy, has led to legal uncertainty and increased levels of successful appeals;
- a demoralised and chronically under-resourced planning service; and
- a much less powerful local planning framework as the result of wholesale deregulation of permitted development, which has removed key controls over the urban environment.'

Publications such as the TCPA's 2013 report *Planning out Poverty*[27] have illustrated how this structural decline has been mirrored by a hollowing-out of the social purpose of planning. National policy no longer has any commitment to social justice and, along with changes to housing policy, any sense of using the wider endeavour of planning to help redistribute resources even for those in greatest social housing need. While it is not the purpose of this book to discuss the rapid decline of financial support for local councils, this has reinforced the regressive nature of this package of changes. For example, in 2015 government announced that it would end the distribution of core grant from Whitehall to town halls and instead councils would be able to keep all locally raised business rates by 2020. However, unless there is some redistributive mechanism between areas of high economic growth and those with weaker local economies, there is a significant risk that mechanisms like business rate retention will starve poorer areas of crucial support, while making wealthier areas even richer.

For planning, the decline in local government funding has been one of the key factors in its demise because it has led to a swath of retirements and redundancies, with a consequent loss of both capacity and experience. Significantly, this process has been mirrored in national government, where the loss of expertise in spatial planning, particularly on issues such as climate change, means that government departments can no longer be assumed to have the right level of expertise to inform and shape policy development. This may be hidden from public view, but it is critical because it means that national government does not have the internal knowledge to know how to respond to many of the challenges the nation faces. Without the right levels of expertise in government we are left without the intellectual experience to manage our future.

What is left of the post-war planning settlement, and does it matter?

What, then, are we left with after this rapid period of dissolution? Do we still have a planning system based on a comprehensible and logical set of institutions, processes and principles? One test of this is whether you can draw a picture of the English planning system – not easy at the best of times, but quite mind-boggling now. Multiple forms of consent, a new National Infrastructure Commission with no decision-making powers, the remnants of National Policy Statements, local plans, local development orders, neighbourhood plans, the list goes on and on. The paradox is that the planning system is now both highly complex and deregulated, or perhaps, to put it simply, frustratingly ineffective. More importantly, nothing of consequence now remains of the vitally important post-war planning settlement.

This settlement, which included the 1947 Town and Country Planning Act, as well as the legislation to create National Parks and New Towns, was implemented by a Labour government, but it was framed by lawyers and Conservative politicians commissioned by the wartime Coalition government. Lord Reith, Justice Uthwatt, the Conservative MP Montague Barlow and Lord Justice Scott were all asked to solve crucial problems of how to democratically regulate land use in the public interest.

The 1947 system was a triumph of that cross-party consensus and, despite being eroded, it has served the nation well. Unpicking the system should not have happened without very careful thought and wider public debate. The 1947 Town and Country Planning Act is important because, despite significant modification, it established the following key foundations of effective town planning:

- the nationalisation of development rights to allow for effective land use control;
- comprehensive betterment taxation to deal with values that arise from the grant of planning permission;
- local democratic control;
- comprehensive control of all forms of development (except agricultural land use); and
- discretionary decision making based on plan policy, but with local politicians having a detailed final say, based on case-by-case expert advice from planners.

Above all, the system reflected the pre-war learning that, to be effective, planning had to be powerful enough to combat the negative externalities of an unregulated land market. Placing the wider public interest, determined through democratic means, over private interests was the bedrock of the system. If the government has decided that effective democratic planning, based on the 1947 settlement, is no longer fit for purpose, then there must be a full public debate about an alternative system.

So where does all this leave us?

Both the utopian tradition and the role it played in underpinning the philosophy of town planning have been extinguished. Planning itself is often described as 'residualised' or 'retrenched', and indeed we used these words to describe it in *Rebuilding Britain*. In fact we were mistaken in this analysis because it is not simply the absence of democratic planning that is the problem, it is the fact that since 2010 planning has been positively set to work against the very values it was designed to uphold. In 1900 town planning was about creating the very best places for ordinary and low-income people to live. Access to space inside and outside the home, and access to nature and to social facilities were considered to be fundamental to people's core well-being.

In 2016 we have a planning system that all too often delivers poor-quality places defined by their meanness in terms of design and space, and even these are affordable only by middle- and high-income people. The overwhelming focus of government's housing policy is on homeownership, with little on offer for people on lower incomes. The result of planning policy changes, alongside government programmes designed to support access to the mortgage market, such as Help to Buy, have seen private sector profits soar; for example, some volume house builders experienced a 40% profits surge in the six months to 31 December 2015.[28] Of course it is no surprise that private sector developers are focused on profit maximisation; it is the rational economic choice.

But the result is that the rationale of planning – to uphold the wider public interest – has undergone a major shift, such that private interests are now dominant. Essentially, the values of planning have been stood on their head, to the point where we have to ask whether the system remains fit for purpose. Today, the free market approach to housing and planning ignores many of the very real challenges the nation faces in terms of climate change and our ageing population, and for all those people without adequate homes. These issues cannot be swept under the profit-maximisation carpet. They are real and they must be addressed, and that cost will fall on our economy. The retrofit costs are much more expensive and so, ultimately, what is most striking about our failure to plan in the public interest is not just its moral bankruptcy, but its fiscal imprudence.

Notes

[1] Department for Communities and Local Government (2015) *Code for sustainable homes: technical guidance*, Gov.uk website, https://www.gov.uk/government/publications/code-for-sustainable-homes-technical-guidance. This publication was withdrawn on 22 April 2015.

[2] Department for Communities and Local Government (2015) *Planning update March 2015,* written statement to Parliament, 25 March.

[3] McDonald, N. and Whitehead, C. (2015) *New estimates of housing requirements in England, 2012 to 2037*, Town & Country Planning Tomorrow Series, Paper 17, London: TCPA www.tcpa.org.uk/data/files/Housing_Req-Final.pdf.

[4] Department for Communities and Local Government (2015) 'Quarter of a million homes granted planning permission', press release, 30 June, https://www.gov.uk/government/news/quarter-of-a-million-homes-granted-planning-permission.

[5] Department for Communities and Local Government (2014) *National Planning Practice Guidance: Viability and plan making*, London: Department for Communities and Local Government, http://planningguidance.planningportal.gov.uk/blog/guidance/viability-guidance/viability-and-plan-making/.

[6] APSE (2015) *Housing the nation: Ensuring councils can deliver more and better homes*, Manchester: APSE.

[7] House of Lords Select Committee on National Policy for the Built Environment (2016) *Report of Session 2015–16: Building better places*, 19 February, www.publications.parliament.uk/pa/ld201516/ldselect/ldbuilt/100/100.pdf.

[8] HM Treasury (2015) *Fixing the foundations: Creating a more prosperous nation*, London: HM Treasury https://www.gov.uk/government/uploads/system/uploads/attachment_data/file/443897/Productivity_Plan_print.pdf.

[9] Thomas, J.M. and Ritzdorf, M. (1997) *Urban planning and the African American community: In the shadows*, Sage Publications, Inc.

[10] Donnelly, M., 2015 'Clark proposes planning application processing by 'alternative providers'", *Planning Resource*, 22 December, www.planningresource.co.uk/article/1377692/clark-proposes-planning-application-processing-alternative-providers.

[11] Carpenter, J. (2012) 'Would privatisation of planning services risk loss of "geeky expertise"?', 8 March, *Planning Resource*, http://planningblog.planningresource.co.uk/2012/03/08/would-privatisation-of-planning-services-risk-loss-of-%E2%80%98geeky-expertise%E2%80%99/.

[12] House of Commons Communities and Local Government Committee (2016) 'Oral evidence: DCLG consultation on National Planning Policy, HC 703, Monday 8 February 2016', http://data.parliament.uk/writtenevidence/committeeevidence.svc/evidencedocument/communities-and-local-government-committee/dclgs-consultation-on-national-planning-policy/oral/28781.pdf.

[13] Bloom, D. (2016) 'Tories slammed for "appalling" decision to push through crucial housing law at 3am', *The Mirror*, www.mirror.co.uk/news/uk-news/tories-slammed-appalling-decision-push-7123668.

[14] TCPA (2015) 'Cancellation of zero carbon homes policy is bad news for the green economy, the environment and society', press release 10 July, www.tcpa.org.uk/resources.php?action=resource&id=1260.

[15] Department for Communities and Local Government (2015) *Notes on neighbourhood planning*, December, Edition 17, https://www.gov.uk/government/uploads/system/uploads/attachment_data/file/488024/15121_Notes_on_Neighbourhood_Planning_II.pdf.

[16] Comres (2015) *BBC Northern Powerhouse poll*, www.comres.co.uk/polls/bbc-northern-powerhouse-poll/.

[17] Bachelor, L. (2014) '£125k for Brixton flat – only just room for a single bed', *Guardian*, 10 July, www.theguardian.com/money/2014/jul/10/125-thousand-pounds-brixton-flat.

[18] Department for Communities and Local Government (2015) 'Over a million more people given the chance to own their own home', 26 May, https://www.gov.uk/government/news/over-a-million-more-people-given-the-chance-to-own-their-own-home.

[19] Local Government Association (LGA) (2016) '80,000 council homes could be lost by 2020', press release, www.local.gov.uk/media-releases/-/journal_content/56/10180/7668062/NEWS#sthash.803ep93l.dpuf.

[20] Walker, J. (2016) 'Government's right to buy scheme "will destroy Bournville Village"', 11 February, *Birmingham Mail*, www.birminghammail.co.uk/news/midlands-news/governments-right-buy-scheme-will-10870915.

[21] Shelter (2015) *Non-starter homes*, Shelter policy blog, 26 August, http://blog.shelter.org.uk/2015/08/non-starter-homes/

[22] Bennett, A. (2015) 'I am English, I am a hypocrite', BBC Radio 4, *The World at One*, 2 March 2015.

[23] Lane, T. (2015) 'Carbuncle Cup 2015 winner announced', *Building Design*, 2 September, www.bdonline.co.uk/carbuncle-cup-2015-winner-announced/5077354.article.

[24] Department for Communities and Local Government (DCLG) (2012) *National Planning Policy Framework*, London: DCLG https://www.gov.uk/government/publications/national-planning-policy-framework--2.

[25] Wiles, C. (2015) 'What is the government's five-year vision for social housing?', *Guardian*, 22 July, www.theguardian.com/housing-network/2015/jul/22/government-five-year-vision-social-housing.

[26] TCPA (2015) *The future of planning and place-making*, London: TCPA.

[27] TCPA (2013) *Planning out poverty*, London: TCPA.

[28] Denton, J. (2016) 'Barratt Developments sees profits surge 40% as UK housebuilders enjoy bumper results while buyers endure rising prices', This Is Money website, 24 February, www.thisismoney.co.uk/money/markets/article-3461626/Barratt-Developments-sees-profits-surge-40-UK-housebuilders-enjoy-bumper-results-buyers-endure-rising-prices.html#ixzz416HCmd77.

THREE

European utopias

This chapter sets England's current poor performance in the wider context of European experience of policy on the built environment, including in relation to the other nations of Britain. There are many examples of utopian thinking and no perfect model; however, an exploration of the diversity of international approaches to place-making and to the values that underpin these approaches, not only starkly highlights how far England has fallen behind, but also some of the possible ways we can put the nation back on track.

World-leading rhetoric

England used to be at the forefront of utopian thought and, until relatively recently, the nation prided itself on being a world leader in a number of key areas. Let's take the 2008 Climate Change Act as an example. It set the world's first legally binding climate change target, requiring the UK to reduce its greenhouse gas emissions by at least 80% by 2050, as compared with 1990. Jim Watson highlights that one of the reasons why it was so successful and ambitious was because of the 'level of cross-party support it received. It was enacted by the Labour government, under pressure to do more on climate change by opposition parties and NGOs.'[1] The Climate Change

Act demonstrated the power of cross-party consensus and the NGO community's being unified around an important goal.

The Act established an independent Committee on Climate Change to advise the government on emissions targets and progress on other aspects of the Act. To set a pathway to 2050, the Committee on Climate Change proposed a series of five-year carbon budgets that were legislated for by Parliament. In 2009 the first three carbon budgets were set, covering the periods 2008–12, 2013–17 and 2018–22. In 2011 the fourth budget was set for the period 2023–27, committing the UK to reduce emissions to 50% below 1990 levels.

In 2013 the Committee on Climate Change reported in its fifth statutory report to Parliament on progress towards meeting the UK's carbon budgets, that 'The UK has met the first carbon budget and our assessment is that we are likely to meet the second carbon budget. However, we are not currently on track to meet the third and fourth carbon budgets'.[2] The Committee warned that 'without a significant increase in the pace of emissions reduction, starting very soon, the costs and risks of moving to a low-carbon economy in the 2020s and beyond will be increased. To meet its statutory commitments, it will be necessary for the Government to develop and implement further policy measures over the next two years'.[3]

In June 2015 the Committee on Climate Change provided a progress report to the new Government in which it asked: 'what steps will the Government take during this Parliament to make sure that targets to reduce emissions for the 2020s and beyond are achieved in a cost-effective way?' It highlighted that 'Virtually all policies or funding in these areas are due to expire during this Parliament. This includes the end of programmes and incentives to reduce energy bills through more efficient buildings, to support low-carbon power investment, to develop the market for low emission vehicles, and to promote low-carbon heat. Without significant new policies progress will fall behind what is required to meet legal obligations through the 2020s.'[4]

The Committee also highlighted that 'the policy landscape is complex and in places inconsistent. Our assessment of existing policies is that some of these are at risk of failing to deliver'.[5] The government has chosen to ignore many of the recommendations made by the Committee, such as implementing 'the zero carbon homes standard without further weakening'.[6] Rather than set us on a pathway to a low carbon future, during 2015 the government instead 'ended subsidies for wind and solar power, increased taxes on renewable energy, axed plans for zero carbon homes, and closed its flagship energy efficiency scheme without a replacement. It also made a U-turn on banning fracking in Britain's most important nature sites, and lifted a ban in some parts of the country on pesticides linked to bee declines.'[7]

Set against this backdrop of abandoning many of our most cost-effective and efficient renewable and low carbon technologies, leaving little chance of the UK's meeting the targets set out in the 2008 Climate Change Act, the UK government was actively involved in the United Nations (UN) Paris Climate Conference[8] in November 2015. Addressing the conference in Paris, Prime Minister David Cameron argued 'why is it difficult to reach a legally binding agreement when in 2015 there are already 75 countries – including countries across most of the continents of our world – that already have legally binding climate change legislation? Countries like Britain. And countries that aren't suffering from having legally binding climate change legislation; countries that are thriving with that legislation.'[9]

Cameron went on to say: 'Our grandchildren would rightly ask us: what was so difficult? You had this technology, you knew it worked, you knew that if you gave it to poor and vulnerable countries they could protect themselves against climate change – why on earth didn't you do it? What I'm saying is that instead of making excuses tomorrow to our children and grandchildren, we should be taking action against climate change today. What we are looking for is not difficult, it is doable and therefore we should come together and do it.'[10]

The current government's approach to climate change, and in particular to achieving the targets in the 2008 Climate Change Act, is the perfect example of Alan Bennett's thesis as set out in Chapter Two. Bennett highlights that language and policy can no longer be trusted, and the above example demonstrates government trumpeting the need for targets and action on climate change on the one hand, while having just actively dismantled the policy support for renewable energy and zero-carbon homes on the other.

The government's response to climate change also remains a clear example of the wider decline of spatial planning. Even after the impacts of successive severe weather and flood events in Britain in December 2015, just a month after the UN Climate Conference in Paris, the government has simply refused to review national planning policy to consider its effectiveness in creating resilient places, despite conducting a consultation into the NPPF's effectiveness to deliver more housing.[11]

Pioneering European approaches

To achieve a renaissance in utopian thought in England we need to look to other nations that are progressing positive and creative ideas that will make a real difference to people's lives now and in the future.

Future generations in Wales

Our Welsh neighbours, across the English border to the west, have taken an innovative and inclusive approach to thinking about the future. The Well-being of Future Generations (Wales) Act[12] became legislation in Wales in 2015 and is 'one of the very few such laws in the world that legislates for sustainable development, i.e. creating a better nation for us for now and for the future'.[13] The Act is about improving the social, economic, environmental and cultural well-being of Wales by making the 'public bodies listed in the Act think more about the long-term, work better with people and communities and each other, look to prevent problems and take a more joined-up approach'.[14] The legislation is about ensuring that Wales is a happy place to live in now and in the future. The Act is framed around seven well-being goals: community cohesion, health, prosperity, equality, climate change resilience, global responsibility and culture, heritage and the Welsh language.

Of equal interest and importance to the legislation is the process that informed its content. The then Welsh Government Minister for

Communities and Tackling Poverty, Jeff Cuthbert AM, initiated a national conversation called 'The Wales We Want' to inform the new law. The year-long conversation started in February 2014 and engaged nearly 7,000 people across Wales through individuals and community groups, as well as using social media and online forums.[15] Discussions covered a variety of intergenerational challenges, including health inequalities, poverty, climate change, jobs and growth and an ageing population.

Based on this national conversation, seven foundations for the well-being of future generations were developed:

'• giving children the best start in life from the early years,
• that future generations need a strong sense of place,
• that we need to live within environmental limits,
• the importance of investing in the local economy,
• promoting diversity and reducing inequality,
• increasing engagement in the democratic process,
• and celebrating culture, heritage and language.'[16]

Each of these values would have a positive impact, and together they set out a framework for building a better future in Wales. Although the Well-being of Future Generations (Wales) Act is now law, 'The Wales We Want' conversation continues.

At the very end of a 2012 summary report by the TCPA, called 'The Lie of the Land,' the following question is posed: 'The choice of whether to engage with our strategic future is a test of our collective commitment to future generations. Ultimately it is also a test of our democracy itself.'[17] In Wales, they have passed this test.

A plan for Scotland

If we look across the English border to the north, to Scotland, there is also much to learn about how they are planning for the future. Unlike England, which has no national or regional tier of planning, Scotland has a framework for the spatial development of the country as a whole.

The Scottish Government sets overall national planning policy in the National Planning Framework (currently on its third iteration) and the 32 local authorities prepare local plans. The four major city regions also have to prepare a strategic development plan. Scotland is regarded as having the most coherent and effective planning system inside the UK, with a strong emphasis on meeting housing needs.

Scotland's third National Planning Framework sets out a long-term vision for the development of Scotland and is framed around four key approaches.[18] Firstly, to be a successful, sustainable place Scotland must focus on both place-making and sustainable economic growth, recognising the importance and need to balance city-regions and towns, along with rural areas, coastal communities and islands. Secondly, the environment is both essential for quality of life and an economic asset and Scotland must be a natural, resilient place. Thirdly, Scotland must be a low carbon place with the policy framework supporting the transition to a low carbon economy. Fourthly, Scotland must be well connected, with an enhanced transport infrastructure alongside digital infrastructure.

The approach in Scotland enables the nation to think about the country as a whole, providing certainty about what goes where and thinking over the long term. It also provides a framework to deal with issues across local authority and regional boundaries, improves the nation's capacity to deal with 'environmental shocks' and, at the same time, supports economic efficiency and reduces social inequality.

Local leaders and global movements

It is not just national government approaches that we should learn from. The European tradition of sustainable cities, led by strong civic leaders, offers many lessons for England today. Following the adoption of the European Union climate change and energy package in 2008, the European Commission set up the Covenant of Mayors (renamed the Covenant of Mayors for Energy and Climate in October 2015). The aim is to provide support and endorsement for local authorities that are successfully implementing policies on climate change. The

Covenant of Mayors is based on a voluntary commitment by signatories to meet and exceed the EU target of a 20% reduction in carbon dioxide emissions by 2020 through the development of renewable energy sources and increased energy efficiency.[19] In October 2015, signatories voted overwhelmingly to have targets beyond 2020 and 'pledged action to support implementation of the EU 40% greenhouse gas-reduction target by 2030 and the adoption of a joint approach to tackling mitigation and adaptation to climate change'.[20]

To date, over 6,700 town, city and regional mayors across Europe – representing over 211 million people – have signed up to the Covenant of Mayors. European Commissioner Miguel Arias Cañete has heralded it as the 'world's biggest urban climate and energy initiative'.[21] Of those signatories just 45 are in the UK, as compared to over 1,300 signatories in France and 420 in Germany. Perhaps one of the reasons why sign-up has been so slow in the UK is because the mayoral model is not the dominant form of governance, but we do have over 350 democratically elected local authority leaders in England alone who are eligible to sign the Covenant of Mayors.

City-scale change

In many towns and cities across Europe and further afield, the utopian and town planning tradition continues to make a positive contribution to society by tackling the key problems faced by the citizens in these communities. There are thousands of examples to choose from, but we have chosen to showcase the International Building Exhibition (IBA) Hamburg because we were so moved by the transformative action the city has taken. We had the opportunity to see this at first hand during a 2014 TCPA study visit to the city as part of a pan-European project on spatial planning and energy.[22]

Hamburg is Germany's second-largest city, with a population of over 1.7 million people. The Hamburg district of Wilhelmsburg formed the project area for the IBA Hamburg from 2006 to 2013, along with the neighbouring island of Veddel and the 'Harburg Upriver Port'.[23]

Through more than 70 projects, the IBA Hamburg has been a major driver for the environmentally and socially sustainable regeneration of Wilhelmsburg, a former industrial area characterised by docklands and industry as well as green spaces. Many of these projects, such as the 'Renewable Wilhelmsburg' initiative, were aimed at securing cross-sector engagement ranging from politicians and civil servants in government agencies to local businesses and the community. The IBA Hamburg brought international experts together with key stakeholders through public participation platforms called the IBA Lab and the IBA Forum.[24]

Among the many projects that have been delivered are two initiatives that have helped to transform sites associated with the Second World War into positive symbols of climate change action. These are the Energy Bunker and the Georgswerder Energy Hill.

As part of the IBA Hamburg, a former air-raid bunker, built in 1943, seriously damaged in 1947 and left mostly unused for over 60 years, has been renovated and converted into a renewable energy power plant and heat reservoir.[25] Not only does the Energy Bunker generate enough heat for around 3,000 homes and electricity for around 1,000 homes, it also provides a place for the community to meet, with a café, called vju Café, having been built on one of the bunker's flak towers.

The Georgswerder Energy Hill is another positive symbol of socially and environmentally sustainable regeneration. It is a 45 hectare former landfill site that for decades was 'off limits' to the residents of Hamburg.[26] Following the Second World War it was used as a dumping ground for rubble and domestic waste, and later on it was used for toxic industrial waste.

The Georgswerder Energy Hill has undergone a transformation. Today it is now an iconic visitor attraction (with over 60,000 visitors in 2013) and an important source of renewable energy, supplying around 4,000 households with electricity using wind and solar generation. Landfill-generated gas is also being utilised as a source of energy.[27]

These are just a couple of the projects brought forward by the IBA Hamburg. Together they demonstrate a wide range of positive activities that have recreated hope in the city while redirecting resources (land

and buildings) to foster a collective future based on human well-being and environmental and social justice.

While the European examples set out in this chapter don't have all the answers, on the whole they offer a much richer set of values and approaches than those being debated in England today. From sustainable public transport systems to urban food production; from energy-positive homes to multi-functional green infrastructure that can cool cities and allow wildlife to flourish; from pop-up pubs to community-owned renewable energy: in our experience, for every problem there is an increasing range of exciting and practical solutions, apart from one problem, and that is the will to act.

Notes

[1] Watson, J. (2013) 'The Climate Change Act: Speaking truth to power?', *Guardian*, 26 November, https://www.theguardian.com/science/2013/nov/26/the-climate-change-act-speaking-truth-to-power.

[2] Committee on Climate Change (2013) *Meeting carbon budgets – 2013 progress report to Parliament*, July 2013, https://documents.theccc.org.uk/wp-content/uploads/2013/06/CCC-Prog-Rep-Book_singles_web_1.pdf.

[3] Committee on Climate Change (2013) *Meeting carbon budgets – 2013 progress report to Parliament*, July, https://documents.theccc.org.uk/wp-content/uploads/2013/06/CCC-Prog-Rep-Book_singles_web_1.pdf.

[4] Committee on Climate Change (2015) *Reducing emissions and preparing for climate change: 2015 progress report to Parliament, Summary and recommendations*, June, https://documents.theccc.org.uk/wp-content/uploads/2015/06/6.738_CCC_ExecSummary_2015_FINAL_WEB_250615.pdf.

[5] Committee on Climate Change (2015) *Reducing emissions and preparing for climate change: 2015 progress report to Parliament, Summary and recommendations*, June, https://documents.theccc.org.uk/wp-content/uploads/2015/06/6.738_CCC_ExecSummary_2015_FINAL_WEB_250615.pdf.

[6] Committee on Climate Change (2015) *Reducing emissions and preparing for climate change: 2015 progress report to Parliament, Summary and recommendations*, June, https://documents.theccc.org.uk/wp-content/uploads/2015/06/6.738_CCC_ExecSummary_2015_FINAL_WEB_250615.pdf.

7   Vaughan, A. (2015) 'Green groups express "major concern" over Tory policies in letter to Cameron', 31 July, *Guardian*, www.theguardian.com/environment/2015/jul/31/green-groups-express-major-concern-over-tory-policies-in-letter-to-cameron.

8   United Nations Framework Convention on Climate Change (2015) *Paris Climate Change Conference – November 2015*, UNFCC website, http://unfccc.int/meetings/paris_nov_2015/meeting/8926.php.

9   Cameron, D. (2015) 'PM speech to the COP21 summit in Paris', transcript of speech given on 30 November, https://www.gov.uk/government/speeches/pm-speech-to-the-cop21-summit-in-paris.

10 Cameron, D. (2015) 'PM speech to the COP21 summit in Paris', transcript of speech given on 30 November, https://www.gov.uk/government/speeches/pm-speech-to-the-cop21-summit-in-paris.

11 Department for Communities and Local Government (2015) *Consultation on proposed changes to national planning policy*, London: Department for Communities and Local Government, https://www.gov.uk/government/uploads/system/uploads/attachment_data/file/488276/151207_Consultation_document.pdf.

12 National Assembly of Wales (2015) *Well-being of Future Generations (Wales) Act 2015*, www.legislation.gov.uk/anaw/2015/2/introduction/enacted.

13 The Wales We Want (2016) 'About', The Wales We Want, website (accessed 13 February 2016), http://thewaleswewant.co.uk/about.

14 The Wales We Want (2016) 'About', The Wales We Want, website (accessed 13 February 2016), http://thewaleswewant.co.uk/about.

15 The Wales We Want (2015) *The Wales We Want Report. A report on behalf of future generations*, http://thewaleswewant.co.uk/sites/default/files/The%20Wales%20We%20Want%20Report%20ENG.pdf.

16 The Wales We Want (2016) '7 Foundations', The Wales We Want, website (accessed 13 February 2016), http://thewaleswewant.co.uk/resources/7-foundations.

17 TCPA (2012) *The lie of the land, England in the 21st century, summary report*, London: TCPA, www.tcpa.org.uk/data/files/Lie_of_the_Land_ExecSummary.pdf.

18 The Scottish Government (2014) *A Plan for Scotland*, www.gov.scot/Resource/0045/00453768.pdf.

19 Covenant of Mayors website (accessed 13 February 2016), www.covenantofmayors.eu/+-Covenant-of-Mayors-+.html.

20 Covenant of Mayors website (accessed 13 February 2016), www.covenantofmayors.eu/The-Covenant-of-Mayors-for-Climate.html.

21 Covenant of Mayors website (accessed 13 February 2016), www.covenantofmayors.eu/index_en.html.

[22] Spatial Planning and Energy for Communities in All Landscapes, www.special-eu.org/about-special.

[23] *Hamburg, Metropolis of the North. Dates and facts*, Official Hamburg website, http://english.hamburg.de/4476362/dates-and-facts/.

[24] Woo, F. (2014) *Regenerative urban development in practice: Renewable Wilhelmsburg*, Energy Transition, The German Energiewende website, July, http://energytransition.de/2014/07/regenerativeurban-development-in-wilhelmsburg/.

[25] *Energy Bunker*, International Building Exhibition IBA Hamburg, www.iba-hamburg.de/en/themes-projects/energiebunker/projekt/energy-bunker.html.

[26] *Georgswerder Energy Hill*, International Building Exhibition IBA Hamburg, www.iba-hamburg.de/en/themes-projects/energieberg-georgswerder/projekt/energy-hillgeorgswerder.html.

[27] Henderson, K. (2015) *Energising masterplanning*, SPECIAL Expert Paper 1, www.special-eu.org/assets/uploads/SPECIAL_EP1.pdf.=

PART TWO

FOUR

Ten ideas to transform England

In Part One of this book we set out how planning in England has been systematically dismantled and in Part Two we set out how to rebuild the planning system so that it meets the needs of society today and the needs of future generations.

In 2016 we no longer have a national or regional way of working out solutions to our problems such as housing need and regeneration or flooding and food production. More and more development is being approved in piecemeal locations, often through appeals, leading to development that is often poorly served by infrastructure such as roads, hospitals or schools. Relaxation of permitted development rights has led to tens of thousands of new homes being created without the requirement for planning permission (for example, through the conversion of commercial buildings into homes), and this means that little or no thought is given to the most basic issues, such as whether there are enough doctors' surgeries in the area or where children will be able to play. We are producing fewer and fewer genuinely affordable and social homes, so homelessness and affordability are blighting people's lives, and the new homes that are being built are often small and inaccessible because national minimum space or accessibility standards are no longer in place. While each one of these measures on its own may not have a considerable impact, the cumulative result risks creating a legacy of poorly serviced, badly designed places that don't provide for those in greatest housing need.

The good news is that it doesn't have to be this way. We need to rebuild the planning system in England founded on positive and creative ideas that make a real difference to people's lives. This requires clear principles and a new set of structures and approaches that can deliver a system that is democratic and participative, and effective and efficient.

In this chapter we set out ten ideas to meet this challenge. Each idea on its own will make a difference, and collectively they have the potential to transform the future of our nation. Five of these ideas are designed to rebuild the foundations of English planning and five are focused on key outcomes that we need to achieve right now.

- Idea one: a vision for England
- Idea two: rebuilding our institutions
- Idea three: fantasy government
- Idea four: a new generation of place-makers
- Idea five: a new planning education
- Idea six: putting people back at the heart of planning
- Idea seven: a new house-building model
- Idea eight: access all areas
- Idea nine: restoring zero carbon
- Idea ten: land and freedom

These are ten things we can and should do right now; our big challenge is whether we have the political will.

Idea one: a vision for England

> *Idea one* makes the case for a vision for England based on clear objectives, set out in a national plan based on functional geographic scales and time-scales based on evidence. We need to regain our confidence in spatial planning and, ultimately, we need a new Planning Act to set out a blueprint for change.

England is a remarkably small country in international terms and yet it is a nation marked by spatial inequalities that hold back both social and economic progress. Bizarrely, we attempt to squeeze the vast majority of our population growth into one small, south-eastern corner of England, which is a serious illustration of the lack of a coherent vision for the nation as a whole. To secure the future of England we need to start with a compelling vision for the future development of the country, guided by a strong articulation of the principles of sustainable development. Although just over a decade old, the 2005 UK Sustainable Development Strategy[1] remains the basis for an effective vision for the nation. We urge government to recommit to these sustainable development principles. In relation to spatial planning we need to articulate these principles into clear operational objectives for planning and place-making. The Garden City principles[2] are the best illustration of what this guiding framework would look like, not least because they deal with the fair distribution of land values.

These principles and objectives need to be combined with a strong spatial evidence base to guide priorities and shape policy solutions for the nation for the next 100 years. The current highly fragmented approach to planning for the future needs to be replaced by a clear sense of what goes where to support long-term local action. There are four key components of this new vision for England.

The purpose of planning

We need to be clear about the purpose of planning. The lack of a coherent purpose to the spatial planning system, set out in legislation, has long been its fatal flaw, leading to emphasis on process over outcomes and to rapid changes of priorities by successive governments. In *Rebuilding Britain* we made clear the vital importance of resource use and intergenerational equity as part of the sustainable development objective. In shaping a new spatial planning system there will need to be a strong statutory purpose for English planning. During the passage of the Planning and Housing Bill in early 2016 there was unprecedented support among the social and environment sector for this approach, and common endorsement of a statutory purpose of planning that seeks to achieve long-term sustainable development and place-making. An amendment to the Housing and Planning Bill, on the purpose of planning which was tabled by Baroness Kay Andrews, explains that sustainable development and place-making means managing the use, development and protection of land and natural resources in a way that enables people and communities to provide for their legitimate social, economic and cultural well-being while sustaining the potential of future generations to meet their own needs.[3] In achieving sustainable development and place-making, the local planning authority should meet the following nine objectives:

- positively identify suitable land for development in line with the economic, social and environmental objectives so as to improve the quality of life, well-being and health of people and the community;
- contribute to the sustainable economic development of the community;
- contribute to the vibrant cultural and artistic development of the community;
- protect and enhance the historic environment;
- positively promote the enhancement and protection of biodiversity so as to achieve a net benefit for nature;
- contribute to the mitigation of and adaptation to climate change in line with the objectives of the 2008 Climate Change Act;
- positively promote high-quality and inclusive design that meets the needs of the maximum number of people, including the disabled and older people;
- ensure that decisions contribute to greater social equality;
- ensure that decision making is open, transparent, participative and accountable; and
- ensure, whenever possible, that assets arising from the development process are managed for the long-term interest of the community.

The objectives set out above would clearly define the ambition, scope and purpose of a new planning system for England. This would lay the foundations for a fairer and more sustainable vision for the nation that would improve people's lives, both now and in the future, and more fairly distribute the profits of development and place-making.

A plan for the nation

A strong statutory purpose for planning must be accompanied by an equal ambition on time-scale and geography. We need to plan for some spatial issues like climate change over the long term, 50 to 100 years, with regard to the longevity of the built environment. The current approach focuses on the short term, and in reality this is often no more than three to five years. It has to be replaced by an approach that drives greater certainty and predictability about our ability to adapt to changing environmental conditions such as sea-level rise and increased risk of flooding and drought.

Planning is a messy business of managing change and we don't expect a prefect process, but a national plan dealing with strategic flood risk and coastal change, for example, must plan for time horizons driven by the science, and that means up to 100 years. Through this lens, the future of England will present some very hard choices around demographic change and responding to sea-level rise, about consolidation in some places and relocation of populations in others. This will be deeply controversial, but there are only two choices here. Either we plan for the uncertainty of the future while we can, or we wait to deal with it through crisis management. There is no doubt as to which option gives us the greatest chance to respond effectively, both practically and psychologically, to the changes that will impact on us.

The vision for England will need to be expressed on that most radical of tools, a map. Maps are engines of change because they draw out relationships with huge political implications that many would rather not confront. From poverty and inequality to flood risk and food production, this new national plan would draw together the best data and help us to reshape England. Technology can now help make such a map accessible as a core part of general education and a focus for public debate.

Space and geography are equally important in rebuilding planning. We need to plan for functional geography, which is simply another way of saying that plans need to reflect the reality of how our nation works in terms of economy, infrastructure, ecology and demographics. At the beginning of the planning movement, Patrick Geddes used his Outlook Tower in Edinburgh (now known as Edinburgh's Camera Obscura)[4] to illustrate the need for a view of cities in their global context and then right down, through differing spatial scales, to buildings and individuals. That is how we need to plan for England, with national, regional, sub-regional, local and neighbourhood plans all forming part of our response to the future. Such a conception of comprehensive spatial planning, reflecting the nation's geography, is in sharp contrast to current the framework in England, which lacks both national and regional tiers of planning. As it currently stands, responsibility for the future development of many key issues confronting the nation lies solely with local and neighbourhood plans.

Regaining confidence in spatial planning

We need to restore the social dimensions to planning practice, acknowledging the complexity of how our physical environment impacts on the human condition. The foundation of spatial planning as a discipline addressed all aspects of the human condition. This means that beyond the basic allocation of land-use functions and control of land uses, planning must regain a sense of self-confidence and purpose on the wider project of managing social change. The field of spatial planning is the right discipline to express the core vision for communities and the nation. This is not, as the rest of this chapter sets out, an excuse to impose the will of planners on people, but instead a signal of the potential capability and multidisciplinary nature of the spatial planning approach. Spatial planning provides a mechanism within which the practical considerations of the economy, the land and social needs are planned out against the principles of sustainable development.

A new Planning Act

The necessity of a comprehensive spatial planning system founded on a clear statutory purpose means that we need a new Planning Act. Planning legislation in England hasn't been consolidated since 1990 and is now one of the most complex and dysfunctional legal frameworks of any part of public policy. We need a new Planning Act, based on the success of the 1947 planning system and designed to meet 21st-century challenges. Sound international benchmarks as well the insights from the now abolished Royal Commission on Environmental Pollution, whose 2002 report on reform of the planning system remains the best blueprint for change,[5] should inform this new Planning Act.

Idea two: rebuilding our institutions

> *Idea two sets out the need for a government department for spatial planning with coordinating responsibility for the development of England, and a Royal Commission on Sustainable Development to provide objective technical data.*

The present planning structures do not provide an integrated, accountable and transparent way of setting and achieving long-term sustainable development and therefore they need to change. England in 2016 – unlike Scotland and Wales – has no government department or agency charged with addressing acute strategic or 'spatial' problems across the country such as housing need, inequality or flooding. England's future is much more uncertain than it needs to be because we don't have the right institutional structures at the right geographic scales.

Institutional changes since 2010 have drastically diminished the capacity of England to organise itself effectively. In 2010 the government announced a 'bonfire of the quangos', with 192 government agencies being abolished, another 118 merged and substantial reforms of a further 171 agencies.[6] The case for doing this was made in terms of efficiency and financial savings but, as we have seen, it made our nation less able to understand and plan for the challenges we face.

In our current planning system we no longer have access to the right evidence and expertise, at the right geographic scale, to inform strategic planning decisions. We no longer have respected, independent technical advice bodies that are needed to provide information and support on issues such as housing, waste and climate change. The abolition of bodies such as the National Housing and Planning Advice Unit, the Sustainable Development Commission and the Royal Commission on Environmental Pollution has hindered local authorities' and communities' ability to deliver on the dual challenges of housing and climate change because they no longer have access to transparent, up-to-date data and advice.

Relying on the local authority level alone doesn't work. This is partly because of the reality that catchment areas and functional economic areas, which are critical to effective planning, do not respect local authority boundaries. The government will argue that devolution will solve some of the problems, but, as Part One of the book has pointed out, the boundaries, powers and accountability of combined authorities can be described only as chaotic and fragmented, and they certainly do not add up to a coherent vision for England.

Here are four steps to providing better coordination and technical efficiencies in England.Firstly, we need a government department for spatial planning with coordinating responsibility for the development of England and the preparation of a national spatial framework. This department would have responsibility for infrastructure, housing, environment, climate, energy and transport as a minimum. It would combine responsibilities that are currently fragmented between different departments, including the coordination of investment on flood defence, transport and demographic change. It would be a big department, but with an England-only focus and with many functions devolved to the regions. Above all, it would have a coordinating brief and statutory responsibility to produce both the spatial framework and a 'state of the nation' report every five years.

Secondly, we need a standing Royal Commission on Sustainable Development in England that would support government by providing objective technical data and analyses of the key spatial issues facing the nation, allowing decisions to be driven by the best available scientific understanding of things like demographic change and flood risk.

Thirdly, the first responsibility of the new Royal Commission would be to make proposals for the regional governance of England. We urgently require a logical and legitimate settlement for our cities and regions if English devolution is to be workable over the long term. This is, above all, a constitutional issue about whether we move to a German system of genuine federalism or some form of ad hoc regionalism. A settlement will not simply emerge by chance but needs careful support and a national debate. The boundaries and powers of these new strategic bodies will be hard to define outside the city regions. In the Housing and Planning Bill it is proposed that combined authorities will have strong planning powers to designate a development corporation, but no powers to prepare a development plan; this is a confusing position and not functional in the long term. Some emerging combined authorities already look unsustainable because of the gaps between their political and functional geography. If London is to be our model for devolution in England, then combined authorities will need the same accountable assemblies, based on the Greater London Authority model, and not simply committees of leaders of the constituent local authorities, which is the current position.

Finally, local authorities will remain the bedrock of action in England, but their powers and financing require change. Westminster has centralised many functions, such as planning powers, while creating new legal freedoms for local government to conduct a range of business, and this has created some conflicts. For example, councils now have a general power of competence that enables them to generate energy, which has the potential to provide new income streams. However, due to the government creating an effective moratorium on onshore wind energy in 2015 and the ending of subsidies on some of the most effective sources of renewable energy, the opportunity to re-municipalise energy has been brought to a halt. Without sustainable finances, local authorities become hollowed-out service providers with no positive ability to shape places. We have already made clear that government proposals for councils to retain business rates locally by 2020 are socially regressive, unless there is a redistribution mechanism. Given the economic and spatial inequality in England, funding of local government must retain a strong redistributive element. Thomas More concluded, in 1516, that rich cities should support their less fortunate neighbours. It must be possible for England to finally deliver on this ambition, 500 years later.

Idea three: fantasy government

> **Idea three** is about developing a Plan B for England by setting out opportunities to improvise the future and making the case for a national conversation about 'The England We Want'.

All of this institutional and policy change has to happen quickly and with public consent. The country is able to undertake transformation at incredible speed when there is consensus about the need for change and the measures required to do so.

The war-time experience shows how the vast and complex administration in whole new areas of public policy can be delivered in a period of weeks and months when the political will is present. For example, following the end of the Second World War in 1945 and the subsequent general election later that year, the incoming government set out a new legislative timetable that included the New Towns Act. On 1 August 1946 the New Towns Act received royal assent and just three months later the first New Town, Stevenage, was officially designated.

Unfortunately we are less well prepared today than was our grandparents' generation. In 1939, enormous changes to industry, agriculture and civil defence were made at lightning speed to meet the challenges of war. But many of these ideas had been subject to planning in the preceding decade by a powerful civil service, in some cases without direct ministerial approval or involvement. As a result, when the politicians cried out for a solution there was already a semblance of a Plan B for Britain.

The current position is very different, with a significantly reduced civil service. In its 2014 annual report on the civil service workforce, the Institute for Government reported that the number of civil servants had been cut by more than 70,000 since the Spending Review in 2010, 'meaning the Civil Service is at its smallest since before the Second World War'.[7] In addition to a reduction in staffing numbers there has also been a loss of expertise and there is certainly no Plan B on key issues facing the nation, such as climate change.

To rebuild the nation we need to start thinking about Plan B, and here are two positive ways forward.

Firstly, the model of improvisation in music and theatre might be a useful starting point. Individuals need to begin to develop a community of ideas by drawing together expertise and community knowledge to think about solutions to the nation's problems. Such a new community needs to start making plans for how government at all spatial scales (national, regional, sub-regional, local and neighbourhood) will need to respond to the challenges facing the nation. For example, it has been reported that the 'Department of Energy and Climate Change faces cuts of 90% to its staff budgets within three years, threatening the government's ability to tackle climate change and move the energy supply to cleaner sources',[8] so why not improvise a new Department of Climate Change, perhaps in Cumbria where the effects of climate change are so acutely felt?

Secondly, we need a national conversation. In Chapter Three we looked at lessons from Wales' experience of 'The Wales We Want', and we think it is time we had a conversation about 'The England We Want'. We should be no less ambitious about engaging with thousands of individuals and community groups, in person and through online forums. This is not intended to be some form of boring shadow government, not least because it has no direct power. It is a project designed to prepare us for the future, a safe space for the development of the nation's intellectual capacity to deal with change, a capacity that has been so sadly undermined. If such communities can produce ideas, they can save immense amounts of time when the politicians finally recognise the need for change.

By thinking about a Plan B for England and beginning the process of preparation we have nothing to lose and everything to gain.

Idea four: a new generation of place-makers

> *Idea four calls for the transformation of the planning profession from an 'old boys' club' into a new generation of diverse, dynamic and inclusive place-makers.*

If you have ever sat through a planning committee meeting or attended a conference with planners, architects, house builders or surveyors, not only might you have fallen asleep, but you may have come away thinking that decisions about the built environment are the preserve of middle-aged white men. As a consequence, planning is often seen as 'pale, male and stale"

Our local democracy is male dominated, with women making up just under a third (32%) of all local authority councillors in England in 2013.[9] Worse still, just one in seven (14.6%) of 352 English local government leaders are women and only 3 leaders, less than 1%, are from black and minority ethnic backgrounds.[10]

Councillor Judith Blake, leader of Leeds City Council, is one of the 14.6% of female council leaders. In an article by Susanna Rustin in the *Guardian*, Councillor Blake is quoted as saying: 'When I speak to a largely male audience about planning, highways and infrastructure, the reaction I often get is that I bring a whole new dimension to the debate ... Thinking about the users of a place and all the different interactions that go on – I'm not saying this is an exclusively female trait but I think we have been obsessed with hardwiring rather than people.'[11]

There is also a lack of gender diversity in the built environment sector. In 2015 the three main professional bodies in the built environment – the Royal Town Planning Institute (RTPI), the Royal Institute of British Architects (RIBA) and the Royal Institute of Chartered Surveyors (RICS) – all had elected female presidents. While having visible female figureheads is an important step in the right direction, the diversity of the respective organisation's membership reveals a different story. According to Women in Planning, a network for women in town and spatial planning, the 'RTPI has the largest female membership of the organisations at 35% ... Behind the RTPI are RIBA with 17% and RICS with 13%.'[12]

Addressing inequality in the built environment sector is essential to addressing spatial inequalities in our communities. The professional bodies are aware of this issue and need both to look at their assessment procedures for accreditation and to advocate flexible working conditions to improve access to the sector, not only for women but also for people from minority ethnic groups and disadvantaged backgrounds.

To help address the significant under-representation of women in the built environment we also need more informal networks like Urbanistas. Urbanistas is a women-led network empowering collaborative work on urban planning and built environment issues, such as regeneration, in more social ways. Not only does Urbanistas support women's leadership and capacity building in the built environment, but it also provides a creative forum for women 'to start and grow their own projects and ideas that help make everyday life better in cities for everyone'.[13]

When we visit university planning schools, which we regularly have the pleasure of doing, the students are the complete opposite of the industry conference description of 'pale, male and stale' given above. There is often an even gender balance, with students from across the country and across the globe studying in English planning schools. These students are ambitious about what planning can achieve, as illustrated by a short film produced by the TCPA in 2016 called #Planning4People – What does planning mean to you?[14] In this film, students from the University of Manchester are asked: Why are you studying planning? The response is refreshing, with one saying 'I'm studying planning because it makes a massive difference to people's lives' and another saying that she is studying planning because she is 'interested in being part of building communities'.

We need to ensure that this ambition is carried through from academic study into the workplace. We also need to ensure that our young planners have the right skills. We support the recommendation in the Planning4People manifesto, launched by the TCPA in 2015 and supported by over 80 organisations and individuals, including over 20 academics, which calls for a transformation of planning education to ensure that planners have the right skills in community development.[15] The Planning4People manifesto also suggests that academics should prioritise research into the social consequences of planning decisions and how they can be improved so as to deliver progressive social outcomes.

We also need to ensure that the public sector is an attractive and viable employment option both for students studying planning today and for experienced planning professionals. We will achieve great outcomes for people and places only if both the public and private sectors are able to attract bright, talented people.

Since 2010 public sector planning has become increasingly deregulated, demoralised and poorly resourced. Research by the National Audit Office (NAO), published in 2014, shows that between 2010/11 and 2014/15, spending on planning and development – including building control and environmental initiatives – has been cut by 46% in local authorities.[16] Alongside public sector cuts there is a feeling that planning is no longer valued as an important public service, with Prime Minister David Cameron labelling planners as 'enemies of enterprise' during a speech in 2011.[17]

The Planning Officers Society, a membership body for local authority planning practitioners, has set up a group of young planners working in the public sector called NOVUS. NOVUS was formed in recognition of the need to better engage with younger members of the Planning Officers Society, and to encourage them to be more active and better represented.[18] In 2014 NOVUS set out a manifesto from the 'coalface of public planning', which sets out 10 key objectives, including:

'• Planners and proud: We have chosen to work for the public to make a real difference. This is our chorus calling for a bolder future for public planning.
• We work for you: We believe in making the fairest decisions for all, not the most profitable decisions for a few.
• Exclusively public: We want the public sector to attract the best talent. We want working for the public sector to be seen as a privilege. That's why only public servants can join NOVUS.'[18]

Organisations like NOVUS and Urbanistas are part of the solution to how to encourage a more diverse built environment sector.

Here are three actions with the power to transform the planning profession from an 'old boys' club' into a new generation of diverse, dynamic and inclusive place-makers:

• Firstly, professional bodies need to actively address inequality in the built environment sector, not only for women, but also for people from minority ethnic groups and disadvantaged backgrounds.
• Secondly, we need to ensure that the public sector is still seen as an attractive and viable option for both students studying planning today and experienced planning professionals.
• Thirdly, informal networks and organisations like Urbanistas UK and NOVUS are part of the solution to how to encourage a more diverse built environment sector.

Idea five: a new planning education

> **Idea five** *sets out how planning can regain its status as the best multidisciplinary degree it is possible to achieve.*

There is much that is admirable in planning education, but as town planning has rapidly declined many of the UK planning schools that support it have struggled to recruit UK students. Planning schools have amalgamated with other departments and changed focus, even changed names in an attempt to broaden their appeal, but this has also raised questions about how much of the planning project they are actually teaching. One of the most discouraging pieces of feedback we have heard when visiting planning schools across England is that they no longer teach the British utopian tradition in any real depth. A lecture here or there is totally inadequate, given that this tradition is the foundation of the moral purpose of planning. Of course the expectations of planning education vary widely, from master's students who are often in work and want practical solutions to immediate problems, to undergraduates who may be as bewildered as the rest of us as to what planning is actually for. At the same time, government has attacked planning by labelling it the enemy of progress. Some tensions, between practice and theory, between technical detail and high ideals, between planners as place-makers and planners as technocrats, are healthy and will probably always exist, but in renewing the planning endeavour we need to inspire and engage, reshaping planning education with the ambition of making planning the best multidisciplinary degree it is possible to achieve.

This can happen only as part of the wider project of reinventing planning beyond the narrow confines of the statutory system, but changing planning education is one our first steps. Three changes must happen now to begin this transformation:

The first is to return to the core truth, which people like Raymond Unwin, Patrick Geddes and Lewis Mumford understood, that to study planning you must have a detailed appreciation of the human condition and human behaviours. This means that planners must study sociology, psychology, politics and philosophy as well as the law, design, art, economics and ecology. Planners must also gain knowledge of the particular issues of our times, such as energy technology, human health and well-being, climate science, technological and economic transformation in industry, commerce, transport and communications.

Secondly, and of vital importance, planning education must include a strong component on community development. Planners need to obtain the essential skills necessary to work with communities: to listen, empower and inspire. In this new broadening of the curriculum we recommend that students spend at least a year of their degree working with communities that face our biggest social challenges. The result would be one of the largest and most ambitious community outreach projects in decades, aimed at what students can learn from real experience and what they can bring to support community action.

Thirdly, any study of planning must begin with the rich utopian tradition that is so vital to understanding where we planners came from and still defines who we are. Planners must know in detail the values and practical achievements of the town planning movement. They must understand its politics as well as its technicalities; they must understand its ambition for the transformation of society.

We should not stop with students of planning. If we are to fulfil our ambition for a better society, there needs to be much wider public engagement and understanding, illustrated by the exciting possibilities of past experiences and a rich pallet of global solutions to many of our problems. Many institutions set up to inform people about planning, like the urban studies centres, have now closed and, while there are some organisations doing this work, the general understanding of place-making is very poor. Planning and place-making should be a key theme of the secondary school national curriculum and the making of neighbourhood and local plans should be seen as an opportunity to communicate the art of possibilities, and not just problems, to the public.

Idea six: people and planning

> *Idea six calls on government to legislate for a framework of equal rights in planning decisions and to actively invest in a national conversation about the future development of England.*

We know there is a powerful and principled case for public participation in planning decisions. This case is based on the importance of community empowerment and learning, of encouraging active citizenship and delivering better-informed decisions that themselves contribute to social justice. The proposals above for a strong purpose of planning and an ambitious new planning framework cannot come about without a comprehensive settlement of people's rights and responsibilities. Much of this book is underpinned by the notion of substantive social justice that drives work toward greater social equality, but in achieving this there is a need for procedural justice, too. This means the ambition for both democracy and equal civil rights in the planning process.

This is not a negotiable request. People want to have a greater say in the decisions that affect them, they have a basic civil right to do so, but the desire for such rights is reinforced by public mistrust of planning and of professional planners.

The literature on participation in planning is extensive and, like many other parts of the planning debate, we know how to organise effective participation, we know the benefits it brings, but often the reality on the ground is that decisions are made with little public engagement.

Like much else in English planning, the current relationship between people and planning is confused and conflicted and requires renewal. This is because planning illustrates a wider constitutional dilemma that no one want to face up to: how much power do citizens have to control their own future? At the beginning of the planning movement visionaries like Prince Kropotkin dreamt of direct community control, and, through the work of planners like Colin Ward, planning recognised, for a time, the case for genuine public participation in decisions. Today there are different forms of representative, direct and participatory democracy mixed together with uneven civil rights overlaid by unequal distribution of political power. All of this is complex and confusing.

The introduction of new rights for applicants in the Housing and Planning Bill, where they can have their application processed by a private provider instead of the local council, sheds new light on the asymmetry of the planning process. This is not simply about the differential in resources between communities and many parts of the development sector, it is about the different rights they have in law.

Applicants have a right to appeal decisions and the community does not. This provides a foundation to planning governance based on a principle that takes us back to before the 1832 Reform Act. Namely, that property ownership or an interest in property should define your civil rights. There is now an active debate about equal rights in planning in Scotland[20] and a growing call by Conservative members of Parliament, such as Nick Herbert MP, for rights of appeal to support neighbourhood plans.[21]

To find solutions, we first need to face a real paradox, which is whether greater participation leads to fairer outcomes. Because political power is unevenly distributed in our society any decision-making forum often reflects that imbalance: those with social and economic capital have the capacity (time, money and expertise) for disproportionate influence in the planning process. So, in seeking equality of rights, for which there is an overwhelming constitutional case, we must be careful not to reinforce social inequality. One illustration of this challenge is the take-up of neighbourhood planning, which has been an undoubted success in engaging people at the parish and local authority ward level, but on the whole it has been disproportionally used in rural and affluent areas, as compared to complex urban areas. We also know that while there is some renewed interested in neighbourhood planning, participation in the local plan-making process at the council level is dominated by established groups and land and development interests. National policy is almost exclusively the preserve of NGO and major business interests, with little or no wider public debate. Since all these bigger-scale decisions override neighbourhood plans, people need to be fully engaged in their implications. Many individuals and civic society groups are largely unaware of policy consultations that last just a few weeks on government websites and are often dull and invisible. To resolve this problem we need to strike the right balance between people's right to have a say and the core statutory purpose of planning to deliver, for example, homes for families on all incomes.

In 2016 we think that there are three key things government could do now to put people back at the heart of planning.

Firstly, government should legislate for a framework of equal rights in planning decisions. This new settlement could be based on the framework of the Aarhus Convention, which is a Europe-wide agreement on people's rights in environmental decision making. These rights would be wrapped up in a new Planning Act (set out in idea one) and would complement the substantive duty of planning to provide for the needs of the present and for future generations. This would mean that all parties would have an equal right of appeal, but only when decisions were made that did not accord with the development plan and only if the party could demonstrate a clear interest in the case. This right could not, however, be used as a veto to deny the right of a family to a home. The tension between conflicting civil rights is at the heart of all constitutional development and there would undoubtedly be tensions in planning. However, they would be founded on a much greater transparency and equality of aims and they would focus the debate about the future of a community in the plan-making process, where people have the greatest opportunity for participation.

Secondly, government should actively invest in a national conversation about the future development of England, not simply through new media but with outreach events aimed at engaging and exciting people in order to get them involved. This builds on idea three, where we call for a national conversation about 'The England We Want', only under this idea we are calling for government to facilitate and provide the resources for this conversation.

Thirdly, government should update the last full enquiry into people and planning, which was conducted by Arthur Skeffington in 1969.

Idea seven: a new house-building model

> *Idea seven* sets out the need for a national debate about providing homes for everyone in society and proposes a radically different house-building model to the current developer-led model.

The facts on the housing crisis are as stark as the human misery it engenders; the number of young couples, families and individuals unable to get a home, let alone take a first step onto the housing ladder, tells its own story of shattered dreams and broken relationships. All too many of us have experienced the 'housing block': an inability to raise a deposit for a mortgage or a rental property or to find a suitable home – indeed, any home – relatively near a place of work.

Good-quality housing, for people of all incomes and circumstances, is a pillar of a civilised society. However, as a nation, we are simply not providing for essential low-paid workers – whose employment underpins an economy on which we all depend – or for people on average incomes who are trying to get onto the housing ladder. We need to build a consensus that housing – including housing that is available for social rent, from either a council or a housing association – is good for Britain. Advocates for new, high-quality housing need to seize the economic, social and environmental high ground to explain why new housing is both necessary and desirable.

There is a positive opportunity to create fantastic new and refurbished homes that meet people's needs, irrespective of their earnings, and to create a safe environment that helps to promote people's long-term health and happiness. However, in order to achieve this we need not only a new debate, but a radically different house-building model.

In Chapter Two we set out both the challenge and the dilemma that we now face in England. New homes and communities must be accessible and inclusive and founded on the highest sustainability standards, and we know that these standards are deliverable as demonstrated by communities across Europe (see idea eight on creating accessible and inclusive homes, and idea nine, restoring zero carbon). However, as Chapter Two highlights, national planning policy and guidance on a range of place-making issues has been greatly reduced and, with our current developer-led model of delivery, financial viability often trumps quality and sustainability. We can and should do much better than this. There are alternative and proven development models that will help us to achieve a much more inclusive and vibrant housing offer in England.

A new building model in England should provide diverse housing tenure options, delivered by a range of providers, from new, innovative and publicly accountable development corporations and local authority companies working in partnership with housing associations to private sector house-builders and small and medium-size builders through to smaller, citizen-led models such as co-operatives, community land trusts, self-build and custom build.

A key foundation for our house-building model is a much stronger role for the public sector. It seems all too easy to forget the significant contribution that planning has made to improving the quality of life of ordinary people since the end of the 19th century. We built extraordinary quality social housing that was an unparalleled improvement on what had come before. In the post-war years the public and private sectors achieved the delivery of over 300,000 new homes per year, with around 90,000 of those homes being built by local councils. From the late 1940s to the late 1960s we built 32 new towns that still house over 2.7 million people today.[22]

Since the late 1970s, figures have dramatically declined and we have seen an increasingly larger bill for housing benefit payments, while neglecting to address the root cause of rent increases, which is the lack of supply of social housing.

As recommended by the 2014 Lyons Housing Review,[23] councils can and should return to a significant role in building and commissioning social housing. There are already examples of this in England, such as the Birmingham Municipal Housing Trust, but we need to go much further. A report by the Association for Public Sector Excellence (APSE) calls on government to change the policy and legislative framework to enable 'councils to build the outstanding, inclusive and genuinely affordable homes the nation needs and deserves. This means providing quality affordable homes for all, not just a safety net for some.'[24]

Our housing building model sees a positive long-term role for new communities, combining the quality and beauty of Garden Cities, as found at Letchworth, with the practical success of the delivery of the New Towns. The TCPA has developed an extensive body of research and policy on how to deliver Garden Cities, and on the lessons offered by the post-war New Towns programme. We now need to be brave and match the scale of the post-war ambition; it is time to build a new generation of Garden Cities fit for the 21st century. For us, this is an obvious part of the new housing model for England because Garden Cities represent the very best of British place-making, framed by a financial model that can pay for itself.

Co-housing and community land trusts are another important element of our new housing building model. These models are not new ideas, but the scale and pace of community-led developments in England is currently relatively small. However, with support from national and local government, development corporations and housing associations, citizen-led models of housing development offer both opportunities for community-based governance and stewardship arrangements and the possibility of providing a variety of tenures within a development.

Self-build and custom-build homes should be an important part of the new housing model in England, and land should be designated for this purpose, potentially as serviced plots. Self-build rates in the UK currently lag behind those in Europe, where the model is flourishing. However, there is a tremendous opportunity to develop self- or custom-build housing at scale in England.

While the private sector plays an important role in building homes in England, we urgently need to create a new building model. In order to do this the following four actions need to happen.

Firstly, government should change the policy and legislative framework to enable councils to build the outstanding, inclusive and genuinely affordable homes the nation needs and deserves.

Secondly, to ensure that councils can deliver sustainable mixed communities the government should revise the viability test, as set out in the NPPF, to ensure that it 'not be used to compromise the ability of local authorities to meet housing need, including affordable housing need, as determined through development plans'.[25]

Thirdly, government needs to be brave and match the scale of the post-war ambition; it is time to build a new generation of Garden Cities fit for the 21st century.

Finally, we can do so much more to support the delivery of citizen-led models of development, from housing co-operatives and community land trusts to self-build. In order to accelerate the delivery of citizen-led models of development, alongside building decent social and affordable housing, government should consider releasing suitable public sector land at less than market value where this is demonstrably in the public interest. It is still possible to achieve good value for the taxpayer using this mechanism; it is simply that some of the returns to the public purse are generated through the wider economic benefits of housing delivery for the nation.

Idea eight: access all areas

> **Idea eight** *makes the case for national space, access and wheelchair standards for new homes.*

British homes are the smallest in Europe and many are unsuitable and inaccessible for a significant proportion of the population who are elderly or disabled.

New national technical standards for housing in England were published in March 2015, with three categories. The system replaces the previous regime, the Code for Sustainable Homes, with new additional 'optional' building standards on water and access, and a nationally described space standard (referred to as 'the new national technical standards').[26]

Research by the RIBA in 2015 into the 'nationally described space standard' has found that 'Local Authorities will struggle to set the new space standard as it is over complicated, costs too much and will take too long'.[27] In a 2015 report, '#HomeWise: Space Standards for Homes', the RIBA found that 'more than half of the new homes being built today are not big enough to meet the needs of the people who buy them. This squeeze on the size of our houses is depriving thousands of families of the space needed for them to live comfortably.'[28]

It cannot be right that some of the new homes being built in England today are so small that you cannot fit even the most basic furniture into them. We need decent minimum space standards applicable across all tenures. These standards exist in London and they should be mandatory everywhere in England.

New homes must be also accessible, flexible and sustainable if they are going to meet demographic realities. Figures published by the Department for Work and Pensions in 2014 state that there are over 11 million people with a limiting long-term illness, impairment or disability in Britain; around 6% of children, 16% of working-age adults and 45% of adults over State Pension age are disabled.[29] Government figures also show that 20% or 1 in 5 disabled people requiring adaptations to their home believe that their accommodation is not suitable. Research by Habinteg in 2010 revealed that over 78,000 wheelchair-user households in England had unmet housing needs.[30] These figures are stark, and they clearly illustrate that housing in England is failing to meet the needs of a significant proportion of our society. We also have an ageing demographic, which will make the need for more-accessible housing even more acute. Accessible design benefits a whole range of people, not just older age groups.

A new toolkit for planners *Towards Accessible Housing* – a toolkit for planning policy,[31] produced by Habinteg in 2015 – highlights that 'the cost of building to the Category 2 standard for a 3-bedroom property was estimated to be £521 more than building to current Part M [of the current Building Regulations]'. The toolkit goes on to reveal that the 'costs of inaccessible housing are wide-ranging and significant. They include: the costs of residential care that could otherwise be avoided; levels of social care that could be reduced or removed; impacts on independent living, employment and social life; falls and other accidents which can be life-changing or fatal; mental health impacts; impacts on general health; avoidable hospital admissions; increased stays in hospital due to lack of accessible housing to return to ('bed-blocking'), etc. Department of Health data shows just one night in hospital costs the NHS around £273, whilst one week's residential care averages £550. So the estimated £521 cost of building a 3-bedroom home to Category 2 standard would be met by just one week in residential care.'

In regard to accessible homes, there is widespread consensus as to evidence of both need and the wider cost saving. This is not specialist niche housing, it is well-designed, accessible and inclusive housing. The need for more-adaptable and accessible homes will grow as our population ages. However, categories 2 and 3 of the government's new housing standards framework (similar to Lifetime Homes and wheelchair-accessible properties, respectively) are only optional, and subject to narrow viability testing set out in the NPPF (as highlighted in Chapter Two).

To ensure that the new homes built in England are accessible and inclusive the following actions need to be taken.

- Firstly, government should restore a comprehensive framework of place-making standards. This needs to include new national minimum standards for housing with mandatory minimum standards for accessibility and space.
- Secondly, government should include a new policy priority in the NPPF that ensures that social justice and outcomes for people are just as important as the needs of landowners and developers. This would mean ensuring that the viability test reflected the long-term costs, or savings, of actions to the public purse, such as the saving that the Lifetime Homes agenda could offer for the health and social care budget and therefore to the wider economy.

Idea nine: restoring zero carbon

> *Idea nine sets out the need for a mandatory framework for delivering sustainable homes, with a new zero-carbon policy at the heart of this.*

Many of the government's policies on renewable energy now need to be reversed, particularly the effective moratorium on onshore wind energy and the promotion of carbon-intensive fuels such as shale gas. Restoring the zero-carbon homes policy would, however, be a key starting point.

It seems hard to believe that in 2016 we no longer have a framework for delivering truly sustainable low-carbon places in England. As set out in idea seven, there are no official sustainability standards for new homes since the Code for Sustainable Homes was replaced with optional technical housing standards and the government scrapped the zero-carbon homes policy in July 2015.

The idea of carbon-neutral homes was formally introduced in policy by government in 2006, with a requirement for all new homes and schools to be zero-carbon from 2016. From 2008 this policy objective was set against the backdrop of legally binding targets to reduce UK greenhouse gas emissions by 26% by 2020 and at least 80% by 2050 against a 1990 baseline, as required by the world-leading 2008 Climate Change Act.[32]

The cancellation of the zero-carbon homes policy in 2015 was in marked contrast to other nations, such as Germany, which has created entirely new industries by building highly sustainable new places. It also ended almost a decade of innovation and progress by house builders and developers in the UK and means that we no longer have a key mechanism for ensuring our homes are on track to meet the ambitious targets set out in the 2008 Climate Change Act.

So idea nine is a pretty simple one: we need to restore our framework for delivering sustainable homes and a new zero-carbon policy must be at the heart of this. Voluntary benchmarking schemes, while laudable in the absence of government leadership, are not enough. Industry needs as much policy clarity and consistency as possible in order to invest and innovate, and therefore a new mandatory framework is essential.

It is possible to develop highly sustainable zero-carbon homes today. They are regularly being built across mainland Europe and they are even being built in England at North West Bicester, although this is the exception rather than the norm.

The first phase of development at North West Bicester in Oxfordshire demonstrates not only that zero carbon is technically achievable at scale, but also the importance of government policy in driving innovation and achieving progressive environmental standards. North West Bicester was announced as one of four government-designated 'Eco-towns' in England in 2009. Following this announcement, those involved in the North West Bicester project have worked hard to make it an exemplar of sustainable development. The energy objectives for North West Bicester have been defined by its Eco-town status and the policies set out in a 2009 UK government policy document entitled *Eco-towns: A supplement to Planning Policy Statement 1*.[33] This ambitious policy, revoked in March 2015 but with an exemption for North West Bicester, remains the foundation for the new community's sustainable energy objectives. The first phase of the new community at North West Bicester is a development of 393 zero-carbon homes, a primary school, a local shop, an eco-pub and a community centre.

To ensure that the new homes built in England are sustainable, we support the recommendation made by the House of Lords Select Committee on the Built Environment in February 2016, which states: 'Government should reverse its decision to remove the requirement for new homes to generate no net carbon emissions (known as the "zero carbon homes" policy) and its decision to remove the Code for Sustainable Homes. The Government must set out and implement a viable trajectory towards energy efficiency and carbon reduction in new homes.'[34]

Idea ten: land and freedom

Idea ten makes clear that we have a proven way of paying for change by the fair taxation of land values.

The land question has been at the heart of attempts to create a better society since Thomas More suggested, in 1516, that all property should be held for the common good; it remains a question of global relevance. Around half of the net wealth in the UK consists of land and property. While much recent work on poverty and inequality has focused on inequalities in income, inequalities in wealth are even starker. Peter Hetherington, in his book *Whose Land is Our Land?*[35] highlighted the desperately uneven ownership of land in England. The concentration of landownership still equates directly to political power, which has largely pushed any debate about the distribution and use of the profits derived from the development of land into the political long grass.

Ironically, as we deregulate public-interest planning, and its control over land, we increasingly expose this debate to public scrutiny. If the logic of the government policy is to give back the control of land to private corporations and individuals, through permitted development, for example, then perhaps issues of properly taxing land become more open to debate.

The democratic control of land and place-making can work effectively only if it deals with the realities of development economics. This partly about ensuring that the values created by the action of public bodies and community, through giving planning consent for development, are harnessed for the public good. It is also partly about ensuring that planning decisions lead to greater social equity. Making sure that we have a fair balance between the needs of property owners and the needs of the wider community is essential. We are not proposing a radical shift in the ownership of property, but simply that the wealth arising from that property should be properly taxed like any other. There are two dimensions to this project. The first relates to the general taxation of land wealth and second to the specific benefit to landowners that accrues from the development process. In relation to the first question, it is worth noting that the level of taxation in the UK on land and property is relatively low as compared to the USA and many European countries.

The amount of value tied up in land is significant and growing, with arable land in England increasing by 277% in the decade up to 2014.[36] The value of agricultural land given planning permission for housing can then increase by a further 100-fold, leaving development land in the South-East at over £1 million a hectare.[37] It is worth reinforcing the point that the 1947 Town and Country Planning Act removed the speculation in land that resulted from these increased prices by taxing the increase in land values. The original rate of 100% was plainly unfair to landowners, but the principle was undoubtedly right. Since 1980 there has been no direct taxation of these publicly created values. A modified form of the Development Land Tax was retained as part of Capital Gains Tax until 1985, when it was abolished,[38] despite cross-sector support. In the absence of a logical land tax regime, planning has sought to recoup some part of development values locally through the complex process of planning obligations. These locally determined rates, known as the Community Infrastructure Levy, or one-off negotiated deals, known as section 106 agreements, have been important in capturing a proportion of land value to contribute to affordable homes and local facilities, but they can be inefficient and they are regressive, yielding most in those high-demand areas that often need the least amount of regeneration.

The value of land is not a simple as it looks. Market values are dependent not just on site characteristics but on the values generated by public actions, be those investment in infrastructure or the grant of planning permission. Landowners do not own the development rights to their land and so the enhanced value that accrues when planning permission is granted should not, as matter economic and legal logic, accrue to them either.

The increase in values from the grant of planning permission can be considerable, as illustrated by the figures above on the value of agricultural land. Whether or not this value is captured for the public good is a political decision. In the case of permitted development, where government is now allowing offices to be converted into homes without needing planning permission, the value is accruing entirely to the private sector. Peter Bill gives the example of one company that bought eight office blocks around London for £30 million in 2013/14 in order to exploit the new permitted development rights. The offices have all now been sold with consent as a housing scheme for £56 million, capturing £26 million in profit for the scheme's investors, and not a single home has yet been built.[39]

We are not aware whether the government is monitoring the hundreds of millions of pounds of financial losses to the public sector of 'giving away' the value of this change from commercial to residential use. A London Council's report[40] estimates that in London alone 'over 800,000 square metres of commercial space have been lost to date, in the process of which 1,000 affordable housing units have been foregone that would have been negotiated' under section 106 planning obligations. The increase in values from converting these offices into homes has gone to the private sector, rather than ensuring that these values support socially vital and profitable activities such as the provision of social-rented homes and school places, all of which would strengthen the long-term health of our society and economy.

So what needs to happen now? The first task is to publish a new government White Paper on land. The last one was published in 1974. The starting point for this new national policy should informed by the conclusion of that White Paper that 'We live in a small densely populated country, so the supply of land is not only fixed, it is also scarce. That makes it doubly important that we should plan to use our land well. For the purpose of planning has rightly been stated to be "to secure a proper balance between the competing demands for land, so that all the land of the country is used in the best interests of the whole people". (Rt Hon Lewis Silkin – Official Report 29 January 1947, Vol 432, Col 947).'[41]

The White Paper should make proposals for the reintroduction of effective land taxation at a fair and modest rate that reflects the needs of both the community and the efficient operation of land markets. It should consider reintroducing a Development Land Tax as part of Capital Gains Tax and, potentially, Corporation Tax. Such a tax could act to reduce land speculation and, ultimately, reduce development land prices. If this reduced the tax take to HM Treasury, it would also reduce the cost of housing land, with wider benefits for housing affordability and quality. Land taxation must ensure a strong national redistributive element and could be hypothecated to support key built-environment outcomes such as high-quality social-rented homes.

Capturing land values nationally through taxation would need to dovetail with capturing land value at the scale of new communities, like Garden Cities. The Garden City model is a mutualised economic model in which part of the profits that new development brings is harnessed for the benefit of the community in perpetuity. This is the model in Letchworth Garden City, established in 1903, which still provides funds for a wide range of community activities today, based on the mutual ownership of the town's commercial estate.

Notes

[1] Department for Food, Environment and Rural Affairs (2005) *The UK Government sustainable development strategy*, London: HMSO, https://www.gov.uk/government/uploads/system/uploads/attachment_data/file/69412/pb10589-securing-the-future-050307.pdf.

[2] TCPA (2016) *Garden City principles*, TCPA website (accessed 26 February 2016), www.tcpa.org.uk/pages/garden-cities.html.

[3] TCPA (2016) *Historic cross-sector agreement on the purpose of planning introduced*, TCPA website, www.tcpa.org.uk/resources.php?action=resource&id=1285

[4] Edinburgh's Camera Obscura website (2016) *The history of the attraction*, The Camera Obscura website (accessed 26 February 2016), http://camera-obscura.co.uk/camera_obscura/camera_history_attraction.asp.

[5] Royal Commission of Environmental Pollution (2002) *23rd Report: Environmental planning*, London: HMSO.

[6] BBC (2010) 'Quango list shows 192 to be axed', 14 October, BBC website, www.bbc.co.uk/news/uk-politics-11538534.

[7] Institute for Government (2014) *The civil service workforce, Annual report 2014*, www.instituteforgovernment.org.uk/sites/default/files/WM2014_Workforce.pdf.

[8] Vaughan, A. (2015) 'Decc faces 90% staff budget cuts that risk UK's climate plans, say experts', *Guardian*, 3 July, www.theguardian.com/environment/2015/jul/03/decc-staff-cuts-90-percent-threaten-uks-climate-change-plans-experts.

[9] House of Commons Library (2015) *Briefing paper number SN01250: Women in Parliament and government*, London: House of Commons Library.

[10] Rustin, S. (2016) 'Where are the women? The "pale, male" council leaders driving the Northern Powerhouse', 3 February, *Guardian*, www.theguardian.com/society/2016/feb/03/where-women-council-leaders-northern-powerhouse-english-regions.

[11] Rustin, S. (2016) 'Where are the women? The "pale, male" council leaders driving the Northern Powerhouse', 3 February, *Guardian*, www.theguardian.com/society/2016/feb/03/where-women-council-leaders-northern-powerhouse-english-regions.

[12] Morphet, C. (2015) *Is this a revolution?,* Women in Planning blog, https://womeninplanning.wordpress.com/2015/04/27/is-this-a-revolution/.

[13] Urbanistas (2016) Urbanistas website, https://urbanistasuk.wordpress.com/about-us/.

14 TCPA (2016) *#Planning4People – What does planning mean to you?* London: TCPA. Online film available on YouTube, https://www.youtube.com/ watch?v=G5fasFZy448.

15 TCPA (2015) *#Planning4People manifesto*, London: TCPA, www.tcpa.org. uk/data/files/Planning4People_Manifesto_FINAL_October.pdf.

16 National Audit Office (2014) *The impact of funding reductions on local authorities*, London: National Audit Office, https://www.nao.org.uk/ wp-content/uploads/2014/11/Impact-of-funding-reductions-on-local-authorities.pdf.

17 BBC (2011) 'David Cameron says enterprise is only hope for growth', www. bbc.co.uk/news/uk-politics-12657524.

18 Planning Officers Society (2013) *POS NOVUS*, www.planningofficers.org. uk/POS-NOVUS/.

19 Planning Officers Society (2014) *Novus: A manifesto from the coalface of public planning*, www.planningofficers.org.uk/downloads/pdf/NOVUS%20 manifesto%20May14.pdf.

20 Planning Democracy (2014) *Equal rights of appeal – campaign launch!*, www.planningdemocracy.org.uk/2014/equal-rights-of-appeal/.

21 Herbert, N. (2016) *Housing and Planning Bill, Nick's speech on his amendments to Report Stage*, www.nickherbert.com/media_centre.php/792/ housing-and-planning-bill.

22 TCPA (2014) *New Towns and Garden Cities – lessons for tomorrow. Stage 1: An introduction to the UK's New Towns and Garden Cities*, London: TCPA.

23 The Lyons Housing Review (2014) *Mobilising across the nation to build the homes our children need*, www.yourbritain.org.uk/uploads/editor/files/ The_Lyons_Housing_Review_2.pdf.

24 APSE (2015) *Housing the nation: Ensuring councils can deliver more and better homes*, Manchester: APSE.

25 House of Lords Select Committee on National Policy for the Built Environment (2016) *Report of Session 2015–16: Building better places*, 19 February, www.publications.parliament.uk/pa/ld201516/ldselect/ ldbuilt/100/100.pdf.

26 HM Government (2015) *Technical housing standards – nationally described space standard*, London: Department for Communities and Local Government, https://www.gov.uk/government/publications/technical-housing-standards-nationally-described-space-standard.

27 RIBA (2015) *#HomeWise*, RIBA website, https://www.architecture.com/ RIBA/Campaigns%20and%20issues/Homewise/Homewise.aspx.

28 RIBA (2015) *#HomeWise: Space Standards for Homes*, London: RIBA, https://www.architecture.com/RIBA/Campaigns%20and%20issues/Assets/ Files/HomewiseReport2015.pdf.

[29] Department for Work and Pensions (2014) *Official statistics, Disability facts and figures,* https://www.gov.uk/government/publications/disability-facts-and-figures/disability-facts-and-figures

[30] Habinteg (2010) *Mind the step*, London: Habinteg.

[31] Habinteg (2015) *Towards accessible housing. The costs and benefits of accessible housing*, online toolkit, London: Habinteg, www.habinteg.org.uk/toolkit-the-costs-and-benefits-of-accessible-housing.

[32] HM Government (2008) *Climate Change Act 2008*, London: The Stationery Office, www.opsi.gov.uk/acts/acts2008/ukpga_20080027_en_1.

[33] Department for Communities and Local Government (2009) *Planning Policy Statement: Eco-Towns. A supplement to Planning Policy Statement 1*, London: Department for Communities and Local Government, July, https://www.gov.uk/government/uploads/system/uploads/attachment_data/file/7773/pps-ecotowns.pdf.

[34] House of Lords Select Committee on National Policy for the Built Environment (2016) *Report of Session 2015–16: Building better places*, 19 February, www.publications.parliament.uk/pa/ld201516/ldselect/ldbuilt/100/100.pdf.

[35] Hetherington, P. (2015) *Whose land is our land? The use and abuse of Britain's forgotten acres*, Bristol: Policy Press.

[36] Hetherington, P. (2015) *Whose land is our land? The use and abuse of Britain's forgotten acres*, Bristol: Policy Press.

[37] Hetherington, P. (2015) *Whose land is our land? The use and abuse of Britain's forgotten acres*, Bristol: Policy Press.

[38] Hall, P. (2014) *Sociable cities*, London: Routledge.

[39] Bill, P. (2015) 'It's all about money, even when it comes to culture', 6 November, *Planning* magazine, www.planningresource.co.uk/article/1371134/its-money-even-when-comes-culture-peter-bill.

[40] Rawes, R. (2016) *Whose Land is it Anyway?*, 18 February, Webb Memorial Trust, http://www.webbmemorialtrust.org.uk/home-page/whose-land-is-it-anyway/

[41] Department of the Environment (1974) 'Land'.

FIVE

Conclusion: time to choose?

At the beginning of this book we indicated we were not sure if we were writing a manifesto or an elegy. We are still not sure. Perhaps it's best described as a message in a bottle. The message is in two parts. The first is a warning to the international community not to repeat the obvious mistakes of planning deregulation in England. The second is an invitation to all of us to start building the utopia that all of our children and our grandchildren deserve and for which we already have the technical know-how.

Thomas More's *Utopia* was the catalyst for one of most extraordinary journeys in human history, a journey in search of the ideal community which became one of the great inspirations for the practical action delivered by the town planning and Garden Cities movements. This book has recorded the end of that journey by cataloguing a period of intense reform leading to the decline of the town planning legacy. Of course we should all have stood up for planning and place-making and the values of social justice and sustainable development, but we didn't. This was partly because of a simple lack of courage, but it was also because the planning system was, by 2010, only a shadow of the ambitious creative force it was intended to be. So, what now?

We have in our hands the means of creating a sustainable future. This book and the countless other solutions that have been implemented across the world show the potential for change and how that change can make a real practical difference, not just to basic planetary survival but to the way we live our lives.

In 1962 Rachel Carson set out two possible future pathways: 'we stand now where two roads diverge ... the road we have long been travelling is deceptively easy, a smooth superhighway on which we progress with great speed, but at its end lies disaster. The other fork of the road – the one "less travelled by" – offers our last, our only chance to reach a destination that assures the preservation of our earth. The choice, after all, is ours to make.'[1] Carson's book, *Silent spring*, was written at time when there was clearly a genuine choice about the future. Over half a century later we are still confronted with two pathways, two visions of the future.

A road to nowhere?

We can choose to do nothing and simply hope that somehow the science and data on climate change, demographics, inequality and diminishing resources is all wrong. Denial is a powerful psychological response and has proved to make equally powerful politics. This pathway is based on a belief in the free market as a solution to all the complex problems we face. We know that, at their best, markets may be part of the solution, but what the English experience teaches us is that, in relation to housing, when markets are liberated from regulation they fail almost immediately to produce the type, quality and quantity of homes that we need. The built environment is a complex public good creating externalities that markets find hard to deal with. Looking after our built environment also requires strong public-interest outcomes and it would be naive to think that market-based decision making will always produce the best outcome for society. Unregulated markets are designed to behave in profit-maximising ways, even when that maximisation is not in the public interest. Deregulation of planning and housing standards in England has demonstrated that a free-market approach will not deliver either the social-rented homes or the reductions in carbon dioxide emissions that we need. In fact the position is even more extraordinary, since private-market homes, for rent and sale, are heavily subsidised by government through housing benefits and direct subsides such as Help to Buy. One might have assumed that this entitled the taxpayer to require good outcomes as a basic part of value for money.

This first road takes us on a journey where the future is uncertain, unsecure and unsustainable. Of course the risks are complex and it will take time for these to become apparent, but many of the elements of housing, planning, welfare and local taxation reform we set out in Part One of this book take us a step closer to realising the great US urban problem. That is, in general, much greater levels of poor-quality places severely segregated by wealth and ethnicity and with little or no way of securing a better future. Such segregation is represented in gated communities, but it has many more subtle forms. Is this vision of racial, social or economic segregation far fetched, unrealistic or impossible in England? It is worth reflecting on how far planning and place-making has already been reformed: there are no longer any place-making standards, all of the government's policy efforts are focused on owner occupation, while our social housing stock shrinks. As a consequence it is now increasingly difficult to deliver mixed-tenure communities in England. There will, of course, be some provision of social housing, but it is woefully inadequate to meet the need for genuinely affordable housing in this country. This road sees housing as a commodity rather than as basic human necessity.

Housing is just one example of where a free-market approach is leading to greater inequality; climate change is another. For more than a quarter of a century we have known about the nature of the impending climate crisis, but we have done nothing fundamental to avoid it. We have wasted time, energy and the talent of a generation of society by refusing to engage with our own survival. Climate change is a powerful illustration of how deregulation is sold to us as giving us choice. It may feel like choice for us now and for the next few years, but our failure to stabilise the Earth's climate has already denied choice to millions of people and will deny the most basic kinds of choice to our children and grandchildren.

The road to a sustainable future

The second choice is the route to a more sustainable future; it is more complex than the first road, even if the outcomes are not that radical. We sketched out a progressive and sustainable pathway in *Rebuilding Britain* and have added to it in Chapter Four of this book with ten ideas.

- Idea one makes the case for a vision for England based on clear objectives and set out in a national plan based on functional geographic scales and time-scales based on evidence. We need to regain our confidence in spatial planning and, ultimately, we need a new Planning Act to set out a blueprint for change.
- Idea two sets out the need for a government department for spatial planning with coordinating responsibility for the development of England, and a Royal Commission on the Sustainable Development in England to provide objective technical data.
- Idea three is about developing a Plan B for England by setting out opportunities to improvise the future and making the case for a national conversation about 'The England We Want'.
- Idea four calls for the transformation of the planning profession from an 'old boys' club' into a new generation of diverse, dynamic and inclusive place-makers.
- Idea five sets out how planning can regain its status as the best multidisciplinary degree it is possible to achieve.
- Idea six calls on government to legislate for a framework of equal rights in planning decisions and to actively invest in a national conversation about the future development of England.
- Idea seven sets out the need for a national debate about providing homes for everyone in society and proposes a radically different house-building model to the current developer-led model.
- Idea eight makes the case for national space, access and wheelchair standards for new homes.
- Idea nine sets out the need for a mandatory framework for delivering sustainable homes, with a new zero-carbon policy at the heart of this.

- Idea ten makes clear that we have a proven way of paying for change by the fair taxation of land values.

When we look at each of the ideas individually, they are all really very modest, amounting to no more than the best of international planning and place-making. It may look radical in England now only because of how low and parochial our ambitions for the future have become. While each idea on its own has the potential to make a positive difference, taken together they have the potential to transform the future of our nation.

The second road is not an anti-market future. It will see a new generation of smart regulation, not simply to deal with our problems, but to create new economic opportunities and new sources of work. This alternative pathway provides the potential for us to change our lifestyles to be healthier and happier. Above all, it provides the opportunity for us to have a greater say about how we use our time and how we can enrich our lives.

Time for a U-turn

Which future will we choose? Even three or four years ago there appeared to be some real choice for a sustainable future. Today, the position is a little different. We are no longer at a fork in the road; we are already travelling down the road to an unregulated, free-market future. We took the wrong turning and have been travelling down it at great speed ever since.

In order to make a real choice we now have to turn back, remaking laws and institutions and standards as we go until we can reset ourselves on a new pathway. This generation has made the lives of the next much more difficult, much more insecure and much more chaotic than they needed to be and now our task and responsibility is to set this right.

Time is of the essence. We know that we have to make radical changes to our carbon dioxide emissions in order to have any chance of stabilising global temperature increases. So the great paradox of our argument is that action is needed well before the next UK general election, in 2020, and the chances of success look slim. However, there is growing public discontent with the outcomes that current policy is delivering for places and people. There is a new fragility in the politics of climate denial, a new nervousness about inequality, and people are beginning to question why things cannot be different. Why at least can our cities not be a bit more like Copenhagen and less like Detroit? Change is inevitable, but shaping that change so as to secure better outcomes requires a new regard for our capabilities and renewed knowledge of our utopian traditions and of our past practical achievements.

One thing we can be absolutely sure of is that there is no part of government, no professional group, no activist network or political party that is about to save us with a magic Plan B. If we are looking for a Hollywood ending, then we all need to start writing the script. The responsibility is in our hands to reshape the politics of change. It is up to us to form new coalitions of interests that will challenge and inspire government, providing the ideas and the critical mass of public opinion to ensure that government makes policy U-turns on the wide range of public-interest issues set out in the book.

However, before the collective test comes the individual question. Do we care about the future? Will we be able to look at the generation born in 2020 and tell them we did everything we could to give them a fighting chance of a decent life? The utopian tradition often returned to the notion of fellowship as a way of describing the cooperation and generosity necessary to secure the ideals of a better society. Those values are going to be important to a new generation of planners and place-makers who will recognise that collective action and the public good are at least as important as personal advancement. Our future depends on the rediscovery of those democratic and altruistic qualities that once formed the ethos of town planning.

As for the future, it is hard to know if there is a critical mass of people who care about planning and can collectively advocate its value. Maybe as a nation we will have to learn the hard way about why we need to regulate the built environment. That said, the origins of the town planning and Garden Cities movement, of Ebenezer Howard's vision for the future, were, more than anything else, about hope: hope for those on even the lowest incomes to live secure and fulfilling lives with access to work and in harmony with the natural world. Our founders dreamt, planned and built the future based on a unique economic model with global relevance. Our business now is to be proud of the utopian tradition, to show that change is both necessary and desirable, and to prove that we can replace the dead hand of hypocrisy with the vibrant challenge of hope.

Note

[1] Carson, R. (1962) *Silent spring*, Boston, MA: Houghton Mifflin.

Index